Millionaire Landlord Secrets

Hacks & tips on how to manage 100+ rental properties working 4 hours a week!

By Jason A. Scott

Copyright © 2020 Jason A. Scott
All rights reserved.

No part of this publication may be reproduced, distributed, or transmitted in any form or by any means, including photocopying, recording, or other electronic or mechanical methods, or by any information storage and retrieval system without the prior written permission of the publisher, except in the case of very brief quotations embodied in critical reviews and certain other noncommercial uses permitted by copyright law.

Table of Contents

CHAPTER 1 Why buy this book? 1
CHAPTER 2 My background 3
CHAPTER 3 Disclaimer 6
CHAPTER 4 Establishing a System 8
CHAPTER 5 Finding the Property 18
CHAPTER 6 Starting Out 29
CHAPTER 7 Turning Apartments 43
CHAPTER 8 Marketing & Qualifying 47
CHAPTER 9 Pricing and Positioning 55
CHAPTER 10 Qualifying & Leasing 57
CHAPTER 11 Managing tenants after the move-in 74
CHAPTER 12 Rent collection 86
CHAPTER 13 Helpers, Contractors, and Repair Protocols 89
CHAPTER 14 Evictions 99
CHAPTER 15 Bookkeeping and Budgeting 104
CHAPTER 16 Section 8 107
CHAPTER 17 Free Vacation Time 111
CHAPTER 18 Pursuit of Happiness 113
CHAPTER 19 Book Recommendations 118
About the Author 119

CHAPTER 1
Why buy this book?

Why buy this book? My editor told me that most people decide to buy a book after reading the first paragraph. I get it, so here it is: I self-manage over 100 tenants working no more than 4 hours a week, and I do this from 3000 miles away on my monthly vacation abroad.

This book is not "Landlording 101" or "A Dummy's Guide to Landlording." There are many books like these already, and there's no reason for me to repeat them. Instead, I am here to provide you with "insider tips" on how to manage tenants and vendors while making money in a very productive and efficient manner. This book is best for readers who are already landlords and are stressed or overwhelmed by the day-to-day things a landlord has to do and the people they have to handle.

What do you do if a tenant is always polite but always late on rent? What do you do if your tenant is not supposed to have pets in his unit and plays cat and mouse with you whenever you catch him with a pet in the apartment? What do you do if a tenant calls you in the middle of the night complaining about a torn window screen or brandishes a gun at you when you are trying to collect rent? What if a homeless person keeps sleeping in your complex and refuses to leave? What do you do if your tenant starts selling drugs out of his back window? What if some college kids move in and party 24/7? What do you do if your tenant starts using your parking lot as a commercial car wash? What if you smell marijuana coming from one of the units? What do you do if you can't find a reliable plumber to repair the old pipe that burst and flooded the apartment? All of this sounds crazy, but it's all happened to me within the past five years while I managed apartments with over 100 tenants.

Chapter 1: Why buy this book?

There are many issues that can arise when managing an apartment complex. In this book, I will teach you how to prevent them from happening. And this is not the best part. The best part is that I manage these tenants all by myself with the system I created. Yes, me, myself, and I. All from 3000 miles away.

My system works so well that many of my landlord friends call me regularly for tips and advice on dealing with specific situations. They ask what my landlording secret is. What am I doing differently that no one else is doing, that I get to manage multiple properties so efficiently? To answer that question, I decided to write a book to share my experiences with other miserable, self-managing landlords. My goal is to help them achieve substantially better incomes with significantly reduced stress levels.

I will do my best to make this book as professional and easy to follow as possible. I will use words like repairman, contractor, and handyman interchangeably. I will also refer to tenants, renters, applicants, potential tenants, he and she interchangeably, so please bear with me. I am a person who believes in doing everything with integrity, so when I talk about my system, I will be brutally honest. Everything I say might not sound politically correct. You may not agree with everything in my system, but it is all 100% legal and ethical, and most importantly, works exceptionally well when managing a complex. Every complex is different, and every tenant is different. Still, I hope that landlords can benefit and learn from my experience to better handle situations when dealing with tenants. That's my only intention in writing this book.

CHAPTER 2
My background

I have always liked reading, and I was fortunate to learn a ton from books written by other landlords. In addition, I have also paid "tuition" by learning things the hard way from first-hand experiences. I was also fortunate to meet a couple of very hardworking commercial real estate agents who helped me along the way. I believe the key to success is to surround oneself with people smarter than you or with expertise in specific areas that you don't have, so you can leverage their strength to help you succeed. Other characteristics I find to be useful for landlords are 1) having the communication skills to deal with people from different backgrounds, 2) having the self-discipline to always do the right thing, and 3) having the heart to "separate" business and personal emotions. To be a successful landlord, one must either have those characteristics or learn to possess them through regular practice.

I had no experience managing apartments when I started back in 2009, so I started from scratch. But as of writing this book in the middle of the 2020 pandemic, I own several apartment buildings, totaling 100+ units. And the best part? I manage all 100 apartment units myself with minimal stress! Yes, without property management companies that would take at least 15% of my profit. I work 1-2 hours a day, four days a week, and go on 2-3 week vacations every month to different countries. I am telling you all this not to impress you, but to impress upon you that my system works. Once again, this is coming from someone with zero prior real estate experience. There is some luck involved, but most of these results are due to hard work and consistently "doing the right" thing. I genuinely believe that everyone can achieve what I have accomplished.

I have never thought of myself as a writer. Still, I believe what I have learned in the past years can help someone who 1) wants to achieve financial freedom

Chapter 2: My background

through owning apartments and 2) is an existing landlord losing sleep at night because they have out-of-control tenants. The only purpose in writing this book is to help landlords out there who are miserable and losing money every day and don't know what to do. If just one person picks up this book and learns something from it and becomes a better or less stressed landlord, I will have accomplished what I set out to do in writing this book.

A little background about me: I am 45 years old and started working after I graduated from college. I have held eight different jobs from IT support at a financial firm, a public servant in a City Health Department, a Database administrator at a Police Department, a Project manager at Siemens, and a Sales Manager at a trading company. As you can see, that is a wide variety of jobs! I guess I was just trying to figure out what I wanted to do. I realized that what I learned in school did not help me at any of these jobs or help me get a job that "made me happy." Even though those eight different jobs had different job descriptions and industries, they did have one thing in common: I was FIRED from all of them! I just can't stand sitting behind a desk for an 8 to 5 job, and I hate taking orders from someone with half my intelligence. By the time I was 33 years old, I had started questioning myself after being fired from all those jobs. Maybe I was just not as smart as I thought I was, or perhaps I was not cut out to work for someone else. I also realized that California was a tough place to live. With high rent and more people competing for jobs, maybe I should move to another city and start over. I did some research and decided that a major Midwest City would my next destination. I moved, and my life has completely changed!

I started working as an assistant in a medical office, where I gradually worked up the ladder to become office manager after several years. I realized that most people are lazy and that if I put in just a little more effort, I could easily stand out from the crowd and move up the ladder. So now I had a stable job and some money put aside. I started getting interested in real estate after watching family and friends buying and making money from rental properties. But I didn't know anything about real estate, so what could I do? I picked out about 15 books from Amazon and started to read about real estate. Those books included topics like "How to find a property," "How to finance a property with a minimum down payment," "How to fix up a property," and

"How to manage tenants." I read each book several times and took notes on things that I found to be very important to use when I become a landlord.

It took me about a year to finish reading those books. I simultaneously started working with a commercial real estate agent looking for an apartment complex that fit my criteria. Back in 2014, commercial real estate had just begun recovering from the 2009 housing crisis and was on its way up. There were some excellent deals out there, but it still took me about a year of searching to find my first property. After acquiring the property, I simply applied what I had learned and turned the money-losing property into a positive cash flow in a matter of months. In the following years, I purchased several more rental properties. With each property, I learned by doing and slowly but surely became pretty good at what I do - landlording. I realized that maybe I had finally found my calling. The rest is history.

CHAPTER 3
Disclaimer

My goal in writing this book is to help overwhelmed landlords achieve stress-free management of their properties that they brought with their hard-earned money. I will share real-life stories of my landlording experience from the past five years and what I have learned from those experiences. Some of the stories I am about to share with you might seem crazy or unbelievable, but they are all true. By sharing my experiences, I hope to help others learn and avoid making the same mistakes I did. I live by a set of rules and principles when managing tenants, and I highly recommend that you write them down. Some of these rules might seem immoral or even "cold," but they are 100% legal, and they help me stay disciplined so I can achieve success. You don't have to follow these rules or even agree with them, but they reflect the reality of the world we live in today. First of all, landlording is not a charity, so if you're interested in charity, go volunteer or donate to your favorite cause. I contribute to the American Cancer Society and PETA every month. Landlording is a business where you need to make a living, so don't confuse it with a charity or nonprofit. Treat it like a business and base all your decisions on logic, not emotions.

Always think of landlording as a business and remember that every penny you spend needs to have a return, ideally at least 10%. Think about the ROI (return on investment) on every single thing you do. Is the money I am spending now going to have a return? If not, do not do it. Think, "This is a business, and I need to treat it like a business," and "I am not here to make friends or play nice with the neighbors." If you want to give back to society, you can donate to charity. Yes, it sounds cold, but that's just the reality of things. With this mindset, and if you follow all of my tips and instructions, you will become a successful landlord with drama-free tenants.

I am not a lawyer or an accountant, and I am not making any legal or accountant suggestions. I recommend that you consult with a lawyer or accountant if you have any questions about the methods I outline in this book.

Some of the methods I will mention in this book might seem "radical" or "extreme," but they have worked for me and kept me sane while running 100+ doors all by myself. I learned some methods from other landlords by reading their published works, but I invented most myself after dealing with vendors and tenants, paying tuition either with money wasted or hours spent of my precious time.

After reading and applying the methods I cover in this book, my goal is that you will work less than 1 hour every morning managing your property. You can then spend the rest of the time doing whatever you deem worthwhile, whether that is spending time with your family, walking your dog, reading a book, or simply lying on the beach sipping mojitos. You will have full control of your time and the freedom to decide what you want to do with it!

CHAPTER 4
Establishing a System

Rental property management is a business, and the best way to run a business is to establish a system with specific protocols that don't necessitate you being there all the time physically. The system should manage the employees for you and generate cash, whether you are sleeping or vacationing three thousand miles away. Having a robust system in place is the single most crucial part of any business, including the apartment rental business.

So what is a "system"? It is a "standard of protocols" designed to handle any situation, a standardized workflow, a checklist, or step-by-step instructions detailing how to run things. The key to having a sound system is to keep it simple enough for anyone to understand, like a manual that anyone can follow. The rules should be in clear black and white. The system I created uses basic common sense and lessons I learned from dealing with tenants and vendors. 95% of the system rules are set in stone, while 5% frequently change for the better. When different situations come about, I learn to deal with them and then add what I have learned into that 5% to make my system perfect.

Why do we need a system, you might ask? Well, it's because apartment rental is a people business. I have to deal with hundreds, if not thousands, of new people every year. I have never met most of those people before, so I need to be efficient in dealing with them, so I don't spend too much of my valuable time. Unfortunately, people can be difficult to deal with. Everyone has a different background and education level and has been brought up differently. There is no one set way to deal with people. So, if I can formulate a system where I can efficiently handle most of the people I meet, it might not be perfect, but it will be "good enough." One harsh reality is that people are the hardest thing to manage since everyone is different and unpredictable. It's probably easier to train an animal than train a human being. To minimize the number of people I need to deal with and better manage the people I have to deal with, I use a protocol. We will discuss this further in a later chapter.

The following are the main topics I will cover in this book:

Establishing a System & Correct Mindset
Preparation & Finding the Right Property
Leasing, Marketing & Qualifying Potential Tenants
Pricing, Positioning & Collecting Rent
Managing, Maintenance & Remodeling
Bookkeeping & Administration
Tenant Turnover & Evictions
Pursuit of Happiness
Book Recommendations

I am an old school kind of person; I prefer to manage the apartment business myself. If I had to guess, using my system, I could manage up to 200 rentals without needing to hire anyone full-time. I do not use any management companies since I think most are rip-offs. I also do not use any management software. I have tried many software options available on the market today, but they require too much customization to help me run my business the way I want it. I have found that a simple excel file and word document will do the same for me without costing hundreds, or sometimes thousands, of dollars each month.

Chapter 4: Establishing a System

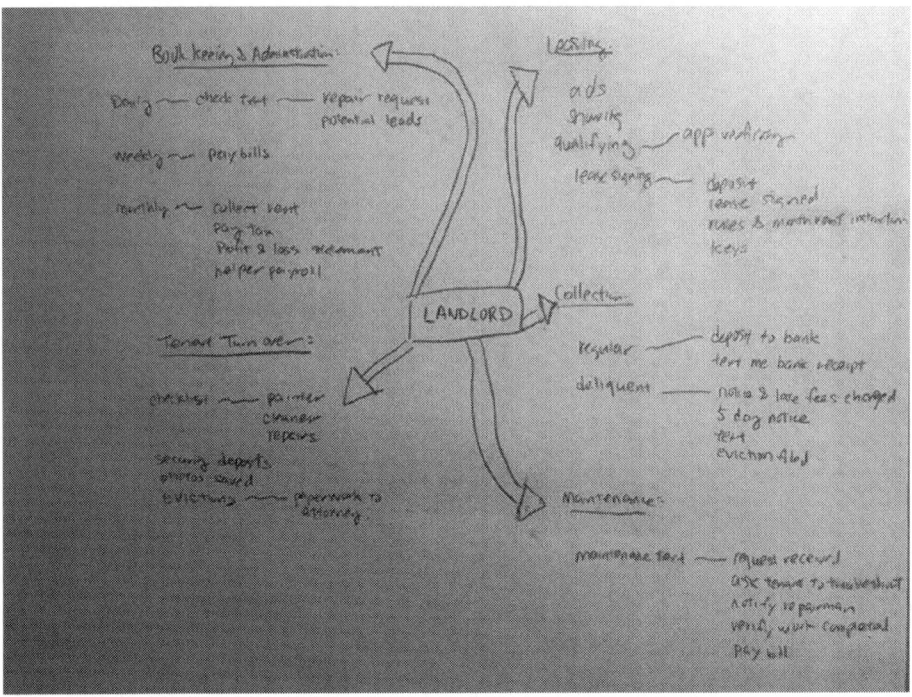

The tasks in this flowchart pretty much sum up 99% of the things a landlord needs to do on a day-to-day basis. Yes, it is a lot of work! But as I will show you, with the right system in place, you will be able to do everything listed here with a minimum amount of effort and time. Many of the flowchart items are self-explanatory, so I will not spend time on each of them. I recommend looking on Amazon and searching for "landlord 101" entry-level books to learn more about the details. This book will teach you the lessons I have learned from dealing with tenants and the principles I followed to become a less stressed landlord.

To be successful in the commercial real estate field, buying the right property at the right price is crucial. You often hear people say that you make money on the buy, and they are exactly right. If you are fortunate enough to acquire a property at the right price, which is 10-15% below market value, you should have immediate equity. But why would any seller sell below market price, especially in a seller's market like we have now? Well, that's easy: many landlords own properties that are mismanaged. There are two kinds of mismanaged or non-profitable properties. The first type occurs when the owner hires a property management company, which charges up to 10-15% of the profits and eats up all his profits. The second type occurs when the owner takes care of management by himself but has no idea what he is doing. He either fails to collect rent on time or has no idea how to manage expenses; hence, his rental business loses money, and he is miserable. In both cases, instead of being a "gold mine," his rental business is just a big money pit. Due to his lack of knowledge, his business loses money and makes him miserable, so he can't wait to sell it and move on.

Since both of the situations I mentioned above are "fixable," this is where the opportunity lies. As a buyer, you need to identify those opportunities and strike quickly when you see them. The key is to be patient in your search. Take me, for example. I have been looking to acquire a new property for the past three years. I have looked at at least 30 properties a month, but few have satisfied my criteria to be a value buy. I made offers on all the properties I considered decent buys, but was either outbid by other buyers or countered by the seller because they thought I was "low-balling" them. But I stuck to my guns, passed on the listings, and just kept looking. It takes discipline to adhere to my "buying principles," which I will share with you in a later chapter, but at the end of the day, if you don't buy at the right price, you are doomed to fail.

I think about the consequences of a bad buy all the time. If I buy a property that loses money every month, I will need to use the money I make from my other properties to make up the difference. I will also need to hold on to this bad property for an extended time until I can make it profitable and put it back on the market to sell. So one bad buy can pretty much ruin all my other successful properties. I can't emphasize enough how important it is to "buy at the right price" to avoid all this headache altogether. Don't go bankrupt due to one poor decision! To summarize, patience is a virtue when it comes to buying a property. Sometimes it's smart to take calculated risks, but don't take the chance when the consequences are high. I will pull the plug and withdraw my offer last-minute if I see the slightest deviation from my buying criteria or if my gut tells me something is wrong.

Chapter 4: Establishing a System

There are two routes you can go when investing in apartment rentals. One is to "buy & flip," in which you buy a property, spend money to fix it up, and then sell it within a year for a quick profit. I know many people who have made a lot of money investing this way, and there's nothing wrong with that approach. However, I prefer the second route, which is to "buy & hold." I think of flipping properties as a good way to make cash quickly, but buying and holding is where the real money is. Not only will I receive a fixed income from the monthly rent, but I also get to take advantage of tax benefits for owning a property long-term. Because of that, it's a no brainer. I save every single penny of the money I make on rent until I have enough money for a down payment on another property. The goal is to own as many doors as I possibly can, thus expanding my apartment empire.

Most people think landlording is the easiest job in the world; you just sit there and collect rent at the beginning of every month. But from the flowchart above, you can see that is simply not true. Landlording is a full-time job, but if you apply the system I will teach you here, you will be able to manage your rental properties in just 1-2 hours each day. You might not agree with everything I will teach you here, but you will be happy with the results if you strictly follow my methods.

Now let's get started. The following are some of the principles I follow.

Never do anything illegal; always do the right thing. There were many times I had to choose between ethics and profits, and I always chose ethics. Never try to save a penny for a short-term gain. I found that if I did the ethical thing and lost money (even hundreds or thousands of dollars!) in the short term, I would always end up on top in the long run. Most importantly, I kept my integrity and never had to lie to get what I wanted. I have had a clear conscience while achieving my success, and that's worth a lot.

Try to be creative; a single task can be completed in many different ways. I am always in search of more efficient ways to run my properties. Don't be afraid to try something new, because you might just find a better way to do things! Take me, for example. Instead of going door to door to collect rent like many landlords out there, I sat down and thought about a more efficient way to do it. Now I am collecting rent at a 95% rate by the 4th of each month. I will share this story with you in a later chapter so you can do the same.

Cash is king. Do not, I repeat, do not ever run out of cash. I know it's easier said than done, but just keep one thing in mind. You always want to underestimate your income and over-estimate your expense by 15%. That leaves you with a 30% buffer to avoid running out of cash. Think of the consequences of bouncing checks and overdrawing a bank account! Your bank will charge you late fees and might even go a step further and call your loans due immediately. Your vendors or subcontractors will not trust you again because their checks bounced, and they will require you to pay upfront when they do any repair work. Your utility company will turn off your electricity and water due to lack of payment, and your tenants will either move out or stop paying rent. That is the worst situation you can be in, so avoid it like the plague. Have extra cash on hand and watch your finances like a hawk to prevent this from happening to you. Cash is king in the rental business, and property appreciation is just the icing on the cake.

Think of each property as a separate business, and never mix one business with another. You should never have to take profit from one business to help cover the losses of another. Each business/property should be able to sustain itself without other businesses' help. If a business/property can't sustain itself, then you should consider selling it and cutting your losses.

Business is business, and it exists to make profits for the owner. All business decisions need to be made based on logic, not emotions. Decisions also need to be made based on the company's long-term health instead of short-term profits. I have had to make many difficult decisions while managing my rental business: what to say to a tenant when he/she asks for a rent extension, how to respond to a tenant claiming there is a death in the family so he can't pay rent, how to handle a city worker who keeps ticketing us because we don't trim our trees every quarter, etc. When I have to make difficult decisions like this, I always keep one thing in mind: everyone is responsible for their own lives and predicaments.

It is essential to define the concept of responsibility. At various times throughout life, one comes to a crossroads where a decision has to be made.

Chapter 4: Establishing a System

Every right decision you make will direct you to a more prosperous future, and every bad decision will lead you to a less successful future. One person might have to make ten right decisions to become a millionaire or ten bad decisions to become poor and homeless. Everyone is responsible for their own predicament and future; I cannot be held accountable for everyone else's well-being. I believe it is my responsibility to run my business to the best of my ability to maximize its profitability while providing housing for the underprivileged. It is also the tenants' responsibility to pay their rent on time and support their families. A landlord must understand this principle when managing tenants.

Before further developing this unique apartment management system, I feel the need to specify some rules to ensure that it is as workable and efficient as possible. The following are the rules I came up with and the reasons why each is necessary:

1. Minimize cash transactions and try to process all payments online so that all records are traceable later on if necessary.

2. All communication, whether between the landlord and tenants or the landlord and repairmen, need to be made via email or text message so they can be back-traced as well.

3. The system needs to be set up so that it can be run 99% by phone. It should not require you to go into an office or sit behind a desk. Everything needs to be "mobile-enabled" so it can be managed from anywhere and anytime you choose.

4. Minimize the number of people that need to be involved. Of course, you cannot control the number of tenants you have to deal with on a daily basis; that depends on how many doors you are managing. But you can minimize the number of vendors or repairmen you have to handle.

5. Keep yourself out of the equation as much as possible; after all, if the business system is set up correctly, you should not have to be involved for more than 1 hour per day.

6. Keep everything simple. If I owe a tenant money, I pay them separately instead of deducting it from their rent. For example, if a tenant decided to repair the kitchen cabinet themselves, and I agreed to pay for the material, I would pay them immediately. That way, all the tenants would still need to pay me the full rent on the 1st of the month: no ifs or buts, and thus less complication.

7. Never let a family member or a friend get involved in the rental business; always keep business and personal life separate. I had to learn this the hard way. I entered into a business partnership with a friend I had known for over 15 years, which turned out to be a huge mistake. There is only one way for a business partnership to end — break up. I ended up having to buy him out of the business because we just didn't see eye to eye on the direction the company was taking. In the end, a long and meaningful friendship was lost along with the business. A successful business is not worth losing a friend over. In another instance, I went into business with a family member, and we ended up nickel and diming each other over every expense and the number of hours each of us worked. Now we don't even talk to each other anymore. Can you imagine losing a close family member over some stupid money? I learn this lesson the hard way. I highly recommend not going into business with anyone you are close to or borrowing money from anyone you know.

8. Never hire a property management company or individual to run your rental properties. A good friend of mine works for a property management company, and what I learned from him was invaluable. He told me that once a property owner signs a management agreement with him, he studies the financials and decides how much the owner "should make" on that particular property. He then works backward to see how many markups he will charge for each expense, such as repairs or supplies. If the total rent collection for a property he was managing was 20,000 a month, for example, and if he thought the owner would be ok making just 2,000 a month, then he would do everything in his power to max out that difference of 18,000. There are many ways to skin a cat, either with markup expenses or getting kickbacks from vendors. This is illegal, of course, but it's a common practice among third party management companies. And when you think about it, it makes sense: management companies are not trying to make money for the owner. They're trying to make more money for themselves on top of what the owner already

Chapter 4: Establishing a System

pays them to do their job. It's a sad situation, but it is what it is. Once my friend gave me this "insight" into how management companies work, I knew I would never let anyone run my apartments for me.

9. When there is a problem, whether it's with a tenant, helper, or vendor, deal with the problem head-on and resolve it immediately. You need to be proactive; the problem will not just go away if you ignore it. Most likely, it will only get worse as time passes. The best time to take care of a problem is NOW.

10. Since property management is a people business, good communication is critical. When an issue requires your attention, spend time thinking about the solution before communicating with the tenants. Most of the time, I can think of a solution almost instantly, but there are times when it takes an extra hour or a day to come up with the best option. The old saying, "let me sleep on it," makes a lot of sense! Never rush to make a decision you might regret later.

11. Always keep your promises no matter what, even if it costs a big chunk of money. Having integrity and others' trust goes a long way.

12. Once a rule is established with tenants, be firm and stick to it. For example, I require every tenant to pay their full rent by the first of the month. Once the clock strikes 5:01 pm on the 1st of the month, their rent is late; there is absolutely no grace period. No matter what kind of excuses they give me after that time, I will need to charge them $50 of late fees and $50 of notice fees, and $10 per day after the notice is given. I need everyone to know I am a fair and firm landlord and that if they want to stay here long term, they need to follow MY RULES.

13. Learning how to be a good landlord is a process; there will always be new challenges. You need to make sure you are ready to deal with any situation you encounter. Also, take good notes when you learn something new to avoid making the same mistakes twice and better handle similar situations in the future.

14. Always tell the truth and be honest. I was fortunately raised this way by my parents, who are both hard-working civil servants. I can choose to keep my mouth shut, but I can never lie. Most of the time, things don't turn out well

for a person who lies. As Judge Judy says, "you don't need a good memory if you just tell the truth." And she is right!

CHAPTER 5
Finding the Property

To start investing in properties, you need to find a suitable property to purchase. What should you look for? As mentioned before, there are many different ways of making money in commercial real estate. In this chapter, I will share with you what I know best, Class C apartments.

Patience is a virtue, so until you find the perfect property that meets all your criteria, walk away! This is especially true if this is your first investment. Remember that your first million is the hardest. It will probably take you several years to save up enough for a down payment on this investment, and you cannot afford to lose it! It is difficult, if not impossible, to recover from a failed investment, especially if this is your first property.

The first step is to find an agent to work with who specializes in apartments. You do NOT want to work with residential agents since that is an entirely different field. I was lucky to find someone who has good contacts in commercial real estate. It's all about who you know in this field. I can probably list the top 10 agents who together hold 90% of all the apartment listings! Getting to know one of them and actually purchasing a property with them is crucial. They typically charge a 6% commission, so they don't make any money unless the deal closes. As a result, those agents are very careful about who they deal with so they don't waste their time. They are looking for potential buyers that 1) have the money to close deals, 2) have experience purchasing commercial property, and 3) will actually sign on the dotted line at closing. I was lucky to find an agent with 40 years of experience in commercial real estate. Even though he does not have many commercial property listings, he knows EVERYONE in the industry. He has worked with almost all the agents, so they trust him not to waste their time.

Since this is not a book about finding properties, I will not go into details on finding the right property and where to look; you can work on that with your agent. Instead, I will go over what criteria you need to have when looking for that perfect property.

The following are the required criteria for all my properties:

1. As far as I am concerned, Class C apartments are the best investments. They are at least 30+ years old but have good foundations and are structurally sound. This type of apartment complex also tends to be more recession-proof. The reasoning is that, during a recession, people that live in class A buildings are downgrading to class B, and class B renters are moving down to class C. On the flip side, during economic booms, the price of all apartments increases, so my C apartments will go up in price as well. At the time of writing this book, we are going into a recession due to the Covid-19 pandemic, but I have zero vacancies! Usually, I would have at least 3-5 vacancies during this time of year.

2. Before I get started, I want to state that I do not discriminate based on race, color, religion, national origin, sex, handicap, or familial status. Who are the best tenants? The ones that pay rent on time and do not complain about every little thing! I found those tenants tend to be hard-working people that work 8-5 with labor-intensive job descriptions. Let me explain. Rich, smart people are likely to sue you over every little thing, and they will complain about a tiny scratch on one of their windows, for example. But people with regular jobs just want to pay rent and live a normal life; they are too tired from work to 1) party, 2) try to find a way to skip rent, or 3) find the time to screw with their landlords. Those are the best tenants, so if you find them, do all you can to keep them! Do this by minimizing your annual rent increase and repairing things immediately since their repair requests are usually legitimate.

3. Location, Location, Location. It is all about supply and demand. When searching for a property, I look on Google Maps for an area with lots of blue-collar working people — maybe next to a big hospital, airport, downtown, warehouse, or freeway. It should also be within walking distance of retail stores, laundry mats, and public transportation, and of course, where there are not a lot of competing apartments around. You can also find areas with high population densities by looking at how many fast-food chains there are in the

Chapter 5: Finding the Property

area. It's a good sign if you see lots of fast-food franchises around because they do their research to ensure a large enough population to support their business before opening a shop in the area. As for rent, I do my research on Craigslist to see what other landlords with similar square footages are charging for rent. Better yet, drive around the property you are interested in purchasing and write down all the neighboring apartments (your competitors) and call them up on the spot to see how much they charge. That's the best and more practical way to find out what the market rate is. One last thing is to make sure there is at least one bank within walking distance of the property; I will explain why that's important in a later chapter.

4. Only buy a complex with an individual electrical meter for each unit, never ones with a master meter for the entire complex where the landlord would be responsible for electricity. I am in a state that usually has 120+ degree summers. Imagine what my electric bill would be if I had to pay for all the A/C units running 24/7!

5. Do not invest in apartment complexes with galvanized plumbing systems. Galvanized pipes are popular in apartments built before the 1970s. They are the worst and do not last! My first property had galvanized plumbing, and it cost me about three thousand per door to replace, not counting the money I lost while the apartments sat vacant.

6. Pick a property with A/C units that are less than 15 years old or ones that have a strong history of annual maintenance.

7. Absolutely no flat roofs! Replacing a roof will cost thousands, if not tens of thousands, of dollars. One of my buildings has a flat roof, and I have spent so much money on recoating and repairs, it's not even funny. The worst part is, every time it rains, I worry about whether there are any leaks or if the ceiling will collapse on my tenant's head and result in injuries or lawsuits.

8. Only look for a property that's within 30 minutes' driving distance. I, for one, do not believe in long-distance landlording. It just does not work for me. Driving 30 minutes one way means driving 1-hour round trip, on top of the amount of time you need to spend at the property. It's too easy to get worn out and become miserable. Don't do it!

All the above criteria are a must for any potential purchase. You can get most of the relevant information from the marketing material of the listing. If not, you can simply contact the listing agent for the property. It should take you no more than 5 minutes to filter out listings that do not fit your criteria. Remember, there are many listings out there; the key is to filter out the "losers" and find the diamond in the rough in the shortest amount of time. After zeroing in on potential properties, you should spend another 5 minutes doing a quick financial analysis, which includes the following:

1. Figure out the CAP using the formula below. To do the calculation, you will need to get the latest rent roll from the listing agent.

Take the monthly rent collected (the actual rent collected, not Performa number) - 9% vacancies - 40% expenses, times that by 12 months, and divide it by the asking price. Then you will have the CAP, the potential return on a real estate investment. Typical CAPs should be between 5%-10%. Listing agents will try to get you to use the Performa number, don't do it! Everything should be calculated using the real number. Do not get desperate and let an agent talk you into using the Performa, or fake, number to do the calculation. Be disciplined and stay the course!

2. The next step is to get the latest Profit Loss statement from the listing agent. Study every expense to see if you can reduce or eliminate any altogether if you end up buying this property. Typical things I look for are management company fees, landscaping costs, pool maintenance fees, trash pickup fees (this can usually be reduced if I call the vendors and renegotiate a better price with a longer contract), insurance costs (approximate quote can be obtained easily by calling your insurance agent and giving him the address), supplies, and administration fees (which are just markups by management companies and can be 100% eliminated). As discussed in the last chapter, the roof and A/C will be the most costly items if they need to be replaced. Look for significant repair expenses in those two categories. That will give you an idea of what to expect once you take over. Many times, apartments are owned and run by "mom & pop" landlords who just handwrite their expenses on a piece of paper. Do not walk away from those deals due to the lack of reliable financials! Those can be tremendous opportunities! This type of landlord has usually owned the

Chapter 5: Finding the Property

property for a long time with tenants that have been there for 10+ years, which means they are paying way below market rate. This means there will be a lot of "meat on the bone" for the buyer. That's the common terminology used in commercial real estate, meaning there are many upsides because the new owners can increase the rent since the current tenants are paying way below market rate.

As mentioned earlier, there are many listings out there. You need to learn how to filter out "loser" listings quickly and make offers on the listings that meet all your criteria. It's all a numbers game, just like fishing: more baits/offers equals more fish or accepted offers.

Once my offer is accepted, I will do the following:

1. Walk the property. I used to pretend to be interested in renting a unit in a complex in order to meet random tenants living there. Be friendly, and they will usually tell you the most important things: what the existing landlord/seller is asking for rent, what is the condition of the units, and if the seller is prompt in responding to repair requests (if not, that means there are many deferred maintenance items). They can tell you about any significant issues with the apartments, how the rent compares to nearby complexes, crime rates, and the tenants' demographics. All of this is precious information that will help you decide whether to buy or pass. Also, use common sense; if the lawn is not well maintained, most likely, the A/C units and roof are not well maintained either. If this is the case, you need to be extra careful during the inspection.

2. Study the rent roll and P&L statements again carefully, ensuring existing tenants pay less than the market rate. This is to ensure that there will be room to increase the rate once you take over. Remember, the value of the property is based solely on how much rent you can collect. If you can raise the rent by $100, you instantly add $12000 to the property's value!

You make money at the buy! If you get nothing out of this chapter, just remember this rule. Make sure you are buying at least 10% below the market price. This way, once the deal is closed, you have an instant 10% additional equity without putting any extra money into the property. Not only does this get you instant equity, but it can also be used as a buffer. What if there is deferred maintenance that the seller conveniently "forgot" to tell you about? Those costs can be significant! Having additional equity can protect you from unforeseen expenses when you take over. Also, suppose we hit a recession, and your property value goes down. In that case, you are in a way better position than other landlords because you didn't overpay. My recommendation is to verify your calculations, settle on a firm number, and then stick to it. Never overpay for a property!

Once the seller accepts your offer, you still have a long way to go until closing. You still need to get both parties to agree to a contract, get the financing in place, do the inspection, and finally sign at the dotted line if everything goes well. Only about 50% of the escrows are closed in commercial real estate; many things can still go wrong before the property is officially yours! That's why having an experienced agent is so important to walk you through every step of the way. I won't cover all the details here about the escrow process, but I will give you some tips and points so you know what to watch out for and what type of mentality you should have in this process:

1. Be patient and never overpay or lower your standards. I waited for three years to buy my second property — do you know how difficult it is to just sit on cash when the real estate prices are going up and up? But I decided to be self-disciplined and not break my rules. After all, following the rules to the T is how I got where I am today.

2. Never rush a decision. Take your time and do your due diligence. Visit the property multiple times and talk to as many current tenants as possible. Talk to the neighbors to get an understanding of the neighborhood. People like to talk; just be friendly and ask questions. You'd be surprised how much information you can glean by simply asking open-ended questions. Make a list of pros and cons. If you still cannot make up your mind, sleep on it, wake up with a cleared head, and I'm sure you will make the right decision to either proceed or reject the deal. Once you decide that this is the right property for you, work at a "lightning speed" to get it under contract as soon as possible. Do your best to get this deal closed asap so you can start making money immediately!

Chapter 5: Finding the Property

3. Follow your gut feeling. Your instincts are always right! Always! Instincts are a combination of past experiences and what a person has learned throughout the years — chances are, they're right.

4. Do a 1031 exchange whenever possible. I know it's difficult to get the right timing to buy and sell within 60 days, but the upside is too significant to pass up. The tax benefits are so substantial that it might even double your profit. There are even options to do "reverse 1031" now. I advise you to seek a 1031 specialist's assistant to get this to work for you.

5. Investing in commercial real estate is like investing in the stock market. Never try to time the market. Stock investors who try to time the market usually lose all their money. The ones that buy stocks of fundamentally sound companies and hold them for the long-term typically end up making good money off their investments. The same reasoning applies to real estate. I recommend buying and holding for the long term. I am against buying and flipping because it's impossible to predict whether we will have a buyer or seller's market six months down the road.

6. The seller or seller's agent usually draws up the purchase agreement. Ensure you study every word in the contract; do not just rely on the agents' or lawyers' word! This property is something you will put a lot of your own money into. Isn't it important enough for you to spend hours or even days studying the purchase agreement? If you draw up the contract yourself, the key is to keep it simple. Clean and easy to understand purchase agreements are best. Have open communication with the seller and avoid any lawsuits if at all possible. Nothing will come out of a lawsuit, and only the lawyers on both sides will benefit. Walk away from the deal the minute you see it's going in the direction of a lawsuit.

7. In a seller's market with few available listings, find yourself a niche. For example, let's say you have 2 million dollars to put down on a property that's asking for 6 million. That would be a profitable niche market to look at. It's too big for most small investors and too small for hedge funds or REITS to go after.

8. During the physical inspection, the inspector will most likely find something wrong with the property. Maybe the AC needs work or the roof is leaking, or the plumbing needs to be replaced. This is the time to go back to the seller and

ask for either a price reduction or credit for repairs at closing. Tread carefully here and don't come across as re-trading on the deal. Commercial real estate is a small field; all the agents know each other, and once you get a reputation as someone who re-trades deals, no one will want to work with you again.

9. Shop around for the best interest rate. There are many online platforms where you can shop for loans with the best rates and lowest points. Sometimes a loan processor will try to get you to sign an exclusive agreement with them. Don't do it! You have the right to get as many offers as possible from banks. Yes, those loan processors might spend a lot of time getting the best quotes for you, and they might end up with zero commission from the bank if you don't make a deal with them. But that is just the cost of doing business; you shouldn't feel sorry for them or feel compelled to do business with them. On top of getting the lowest interest rate and the best terms, apply for a non-recourse loan and try to get the longest loan term possible. Extending the loan to 30 years vs. 20 years can reduce your monthly financial obligation significantly. Remember, time is your friend when you are a long-term buy and hold investor. The goal is to take home as much money as possible, and a longer-term loan will help you achieve that. Another piece of advice is to read the fine print and review the contract carefully before you sign on the dotted line. I recently refinanced one of my apartments from a 5-year loan to a ten-year loan. The bank promised me that I'd get a better rate, so I trusted him and signed the paperwork without carefully reviewing it. You can guess what happened. Instead of my rate decreasing, it went from 4.1 to 4.25! Once I realized what had happened, I tried calling my banker, and guess what, he had moved on to another bank. This one is on me, a tough lesson I will never forget!

10. Negotiate with the title company. Scrutinize every single item you see on the closing statement. 50% of the charges are just made up. Everything is negotiable, even the closing fees. Asking for an investor's discount can save you a lot of money. Remember that this is a zero-sum game, and the bank's job is to squeeze as much money out of you as possible. They figure that because this is a multi-million-dollar loan, the seller won't care or pay attention to "little fees." Hence, they take advantage of the situation and add as many fees as possible. Don't be that sucker! The Title Company is NOT on your side; they are there to make money, so be a "hard-ass" and eliminate as many fees as you can. I heard from a friend that his title company once added some

Chapter 5: Finding the Property

frivolous fees at the very last minute before closing. So review everything carefully before signing on the dotted line. It's a jungle out there, and you'd better watch yourself.

11. Try to set some cash aside as an emergency fund. You want to be ready for a rainy day. And always remember that the bank will show you no mercy. Once your loan payment is late, they have the right to take your property away the very next day. Don't let that happen to you.

12. Spend some time planning out your money and resources, and don't overextend yourself. Landlording is not an easy job, especially for the first 3-4 months after taking over the property, so be ready mentally and physically for the long hours.

13. When negotiating the final price with the seller, don't be afraid to submit a low-ball offer. You might just get it! Some people say you shouldn't piss off a seller to the point where he won't even counter your offer. I disagree. I think the reward outweighs the risks, so I will keep doing it. Also, that's why it's important to have an experienced agent on your side who can soften the blow for you. Always remember that the seller put his property on the market because he wants to sell it, and he has as much at stake as you, so don't be afraid to low ball him. I always have a bottom-line number in mind before I go into any negotiation, and I would never cross that red line. Never tell anyone what that number is, not even your own agent! They should be out there getting you the best price possible. In addition to being able to walk away from a deal, the other thing I have learned about getting the best deal is to have the right mentality. Keep in mind that there are always other deals out there, so don't "care too much" about one particular option. Remember that the one that cares the least will tend to have the upper hand and thus end up with better prices and terms. There are also times where there's another bid on the same listing. Whenever that happens, I wait to make another offer on the property. Never, ever get into a bidding war with another buyer. It does not make sense because you will most likely overpay for a property, and that's just not worth it.

14. Build a team of experts around you. The team should include a certified public accountant, an attorney specializing in contracts and real estate, and a

commercial real estate agent or broker. Remember, you are only as good as your team. I was fortunate to have the best team members, all elite in their perspective fields. My CPA charges 30% more per hour than other regular CPAs, but that's nothing compared to the taxes he has saved me. My attorney helped me avoid some major mistakes in contract negotiation, and he also charges significantly higher than others. But both of them are worth every single penny! My real estate agent is also great! He has over 40 years of experience in the commercial real estate industry. He has also owned both apartments and retail complexes, so he has hands-on knowledge of what it takes to be a landlord. Also, since he has been in the field for such a long time, he knows everyone in commercial real estate, which is essential. As I mentioned before, commercial real estate is a very small industry with only a handful of agents that control 95% of the listings. You have to be in that small circle, or else those listing agents will not even take your calls. I interviewed many agents before I was fortunate enough to find the one I work with now. When I first started, I found a couple of potential deals and almost got them under contract, but my agent talked me out of it. The agent doesn't make a dime until I buy, yet he actually talked me out of deals that would have given him hefty commissions! At that point, I knew I had an agent who was looking out for me and had my best interests in mind. In return, I have been very loyal to him, involving him with every single deal I have been a part of and not doing anything without his OK. A couple of times, the listing agent wanted to double-dip on both sides so they could get the full 6% commission. Even though those were good deals where I could make a substantial profit, I turned them down because I wanted my agent to get his 3%! Now that's trust! Once again, it's important to have those three experts to advise you along the way. They are not that easy to find, but the trick is to ask them for referrals. For example, if you are lucky enough to find a good CPA, ask him to refer a good broker or attorney to you. You know the saying "birds of a feather flock together." It is true! One good professional knows who the other good professionals are, so don't be shy to ask!

15. Never borrow money for the down payment, especially if this is your first deal. I have heard of people borrowing against their credit cards, using hard cash, or even taking out loans on their houses to get enough money to get started in buying commercial real estate properties. This is a risky gamble! Instead of buying an expensive complex with 30 units, you should look for

Chapter 5: Finding the Property

something on a smaller scale to get started. Maybe a duplex or fourplex. Remember, you are learning as you go. Since this is your first investment, the odds are against you. You don't want to lose your shirt in the meantime! Be conservative and play it safe. Wait until you save up enough money for a down payment and look for a smaller complex before going all-in on something bigger.

16. Having the right mix of units is essential. I recommend the following: 50% one-bedroom, 25% two-bedroom, 25% three bedrooms. This way, you are offering something for everyone. And of course, the bigger each unit, the better. Some of my one-bedrooms are 800 square feet and could easily be converted to two-bedrooms; I would simply have to add some drywall to divide up the big one bedroom into two. It's always good to have options.

17. I have walked away from deals before during the negotiation process after realizing that the seller was not negotiating in good faith. Once I realized that I was not dealing with the right people, I trusted my gut and walked away from the deal. I saved myself a lot of time by not dealing with someone who was not being honest or displaying any integrity! The deal would most likely have fallen apart anyway since they would not have honored what we agreed on. I always negotiate in good faith, and I expect others to do the same. You have the right to walk away if you see something different.

CHAPTER 6
Starting Out

So now you have officially taken over the property. There are many things you need to do right away to turn this property into a cash cow. Some people take a whole year to get the property up to the point where it's generating a decent monthly income. I do it a little differently; it usually takes me a little over two months to get the property to where it's generating maximum monthly profit. I recommend that you read this section carefully and take good notes! The tips I cover below will benefit you for years to come.

After taking over a property, the things you need to do fall into the following four major categories, listed in the order of priority.

1. Rebranding & Remodeling
2. Meet the tenant/customers and get them to sign the new lease
3. Cut expenses
4. Raise the rent to market value & get rid of "bad tenants"
5. Set up a system of protocols to follow

Let's get right into it. The first step is to rebrand and remodel the complex. The goal of doing this is to change the complex's appearance to that of an upgraded property and give you a reason to raise the rent to the market rate. First, identify what you want to do physically to the building:

1. Paint the building a darker color such as brown or grey. Use semi-gloss paint to make it more dirt resistant. Paint the doors and window trim as well, if possible. You'd be surprised what a little paint job can do for a building!

2. Replace anything that tenants will see or touch. This includes doorknobs, mailboxes, and kitchen and bathroom faucets. Install a water-saving

showerhead, replace all carpets with ceramic tile flooring, install plastic electrical plates (50 cents each), and update the little signage displays showing the unit numbers. Everything listed here can be done within a budget and will completely change the impression of the building.

3. Change the name of the complex. I recommend using the major cross streets — Jefferson 24th Apartments, for example. Renaming the complex does two things: first, it lets the neighbors (your potential tenants) know that there has been a change of ownership; second, it shows the existing tenants that you are making changes, thus giving them a subtle hint that the rent is about to go up.

4. Put new signage out there. Use a real estate sign made out of wood that attaches to cement underground. Make sure to use a bright yellow color for the background and a vivid red color for the text. The sign should be big and easy to read by passing cars. It should have the new complex's name, the words "FOR RENT," and your text-now app phone number. This is the most effective marketing you can invest in for your complex! Most of your potential tenants already live close by, and most likely, they see your complex driving home from work. The sign they see every day gives them the idea of moving to your complex once their existing lease is up. Banners showing availability are also good. I don't use them personally because I think it's too much work to hang them high off the ground, but you can definitely use banners if you have the time, anything to attract eyeballs!

 The second step is to meet the tenants and introduce yourself. First, draw up a new month-to-month lease, and then visit every single tenant to introduce yourself. The script will go something like this: "Hi, My name is Mr. Jones. I am the new property manager, and I want to let you know that there has been a change of ownership for this apartment complex. I just wanted to meet you and introduce myself. Everything will stay the same, but we do have to sign a new lease. If I can have you sign right here…" (present the tenant the prepared lease to sign). "Ok, there will be some new rules, and I have listed them here for you." (Present the tenant the house rules). "The most important part is that rent is due on the 1st of the month or before; there is no more grace period. So once the clock hits 5:01 pm, there will be $100 of late and notice fees. There are no exceptions. So please pay your rent on time." (Present the tenant the rent-paying instructions). For landlords that find the above script difficult to follow, I provide a more detailed step-by-step version and sample documents below.

There are many lease templates online. I recommend consulting with your attorney and use a lease that's best suited for your particular rental property. One thing I do suggest is to only sign month-to-month leases with your tenants. Some of you might ask why use month-to-month leases instead of 12 month or 6-month leases? I gave this a lot of thought when I started out and even made up a pros and cons list after talking to several eviction attorneys. The conclusion is that the pros of using month-to-month leases outweigh the cons. Say the tenant wants to move out for whatever reason. Having a longer-term lease will not prevent them from moving out; it is just not part of their consideration. Half of them don't understand the concept of a contract, and the other half just don't care. So landlords who think that long-term leases will hold tenants in place are sadly misinformed. From the landlord's perspective, having that long-term lease does nothing for them. But there are many benefits to having a month-to-month lease. During a tenant's tenancy in a month-to-month lease, the landlord has the option to give a 30-day non-renewal notice, which means the landlord can ask the tenant to leave after 30 days without giving a reason. This is an excellent weapon for the landlord. For example, suppose a new tenant starts generating a lot of traffic around his house (aka trafficking drugs). In that case, the landlord does not need any proof to get rid of them; just give them a 30 days' notice to move out. It's that simple. Or suppose the tenant becomes a troublemaker, for example playing loud music at night or having a pet in his unit without the landlord's permission. Those violations would be hard to prove in court. Having the option to give a 30-day non-renewal notice will save the landlord a lot of headache and time. From this perspective, the pros of having a month-to-month lease outweigh the pros of having a 12-month lease. There is only one exception to this rule. When you want to put this listing on the market, it's better to have a 12-month lease. Most buyers are not experienced with month-to-month leases, and they prefer to see a long-term lease in place, thinking it makes the property "more stable." Also, lenders generally like to see long-term leases as well. I won't go into all the details of why that is, but from my years of experience running my properties, I know that month-to-month leases are the only way to go.

Chapter 6: Starting Out

Once the tenants sign the new month-to-month lease, you can present the new "house rules." It's important to let all the tenants know the ground rules at the very beginning. This is what I would say to the tenants: "Mr. Smith, now that you have signed the lease, I will go over the Rules we have implemented for our community to ensure we are providing the best environment possible for the people living here."

The following is a sample of some "house rules" I use for my tenants. It also includes tenant instructions on how to pay the monthly rent.

Millionaire Landlord Secrets

Tenant Rules & Rent Instruction

-Rent is due <u>on or before the 1st of the month</u>. There is NO GRACE PERIOD. So it's considered late by 5:01pm on 1st of the month, you will be charge $100 fees plus $10 per day starting on 2nd of the month. Eviction will be filed shortly after, so PAY YOUR RENT ON TIME!

-We do not accept rent at our office. Please go to any Bank branch to <u>pay your rent on or before 1st of the month</u>. Please turn to the back page for a sample of deposit slip and the account information. You will need to do the following:

    1) Write your <u>name and apartment number</u> on the deposit slip and text it to (555)555-1234
    2) Write your <u>name and apartment number</u> on the receipt and text it to (555)555-1234

-This is a quiet family oriented community, so NO PETS, NO LOUD MUSIC, NO PARTIES, NO LOITERING, this is your home from now it, please keep the yard and parking area CLEAN as you would with your own home.

-Your unit will come with a gas or electric stove. You will need to buy your own refrigerator. An use refrigerator in good condition will cost about $120-150, I can provide contact if needed. If your unit already comes with a fridge that is left there by the previous tenant. If you decide to keep the fridge, you will be solely responsible for any issues or repairs.

-If any repair is needed, please take a picture <u>and</u> video of your concern and text it to (555)555-1234. Please note you will be charged for the repair if you cause the damage.

<u>AC Issue Troubleshoot:</u> 1) check there's new battery in the thermostat, 2) there's a new air filter, 3) turn the AC off for 30 minutes and turn it back on, 4)thermometer is set above room temperature of 76 degrees. Remember, you need to pay $150 trip charge if the repairman shows up and there's nothing wrong with your AC.

<u>Pluming Issues Troubleshoot:</u> Do NOT flush big items such as baby diapers, thick toilet paper, or tampon down the toilet, or you will clog up your drain. Always use a Sink Strainer/Drain Filter in your bathtub, bathroom and kitchen sink. Always use shower curtain when taking shower. When your sink is clogged, please try using Drano or plunger to clear up the clog. Remember, you receive this unit with cleared line, so when you cause the clog, you need to unclog it yourself. You can call and pay the plumber yourself, it should cost about $100-$150. <u>Do NOT call the landlord</u> as it is your responsibility.

<u>Broken Windows:</u> $100 per window.

<u>Lockout & keys policy:</u> You are supposed to leave a spare key with your friends or neighbors close by, someone that you trust, so they can help you gain access to your own unit when you lock yourself out. Do not contact the landlord to unlock your door for you. Also, you can not change door lock without landlord's permission, that's ground for immediate termination of lease.

Chapter 6: Starting Out

Most of those rules are straight forward: no noise, no loud parties, troubleshoot problems before calling for repairs (this is important, and I'll go into more detail in a later chapter), zero tolerance for paying rent late, and the no pets policy. For those of you considering accepting pets and either just collecting higher pet deposits or a pet rent: Don't Do It! Once again, the cons outweigh the pros. I once allowed tenants to have pets when I first became a landlord, and I totally regretted it. I am a pet lover myself, but this is a book to protect landlords, and here's the truth of the matter: the smell of a cat and dog urine is impossible to remove. I have ceramic tile floorings for all my apartment units due to their durability and affordability. Still, dog urine gets into the grout between the tiles, and you simply cannot get it out! I have tried soaking the whole floor in bleach and different chemicals I bought on Amazon, and nothing works. I ended up having to change the flooring for the entire unit, which cost me over a thousand dollars. I also spent over a month dealing with this issue and promised myself that I would never go through this again. Pets will destroy blinds and scratch walls sometimes, making units costly to turn. Trust me when I say that no deposit or amount of pet rent is worth it! From that time forward, I implemented a strict no-pet policy for all my apartments. As for the other rules I list above, I will go through them in more detail in later chapters.

Once you have reviewed the house rules with the tenant, you can go over how they can pay their monthly rent. We ask them not to come to the office to pay rent; instead, they should go to a bank to directly pay rent to the landlord's bank account. 90% of the landlords I know would knock on the tenant's door, trying to collect rent on the first of the month. What happens is that tenants who don't have the full rent would pretend not to be home. It's a cat and mouse game and a major headache! I am going to eliminate this hassle for you here altogether. It is not the landlord's responsibility to chase down tenants to pay rent; on the contrary, it's the tenants' responsibility to pay rent on time. You already signed a lease stating that tenants would pay rent on the 1st of each month, and you should expect the tenants to abide by all terms in the lease without having to chase after them. So on or before the 1st of every month, the tenants need to go to the local bank (which is within walking distance) and pay their rent. No excuses from the tenant and no hassles for the landlord. It's a win-win.

At the end of your visit with the tenant, make sure to say the following: "Do you understand all the rules I have explained to you?" (yes) "Ok, good." To me, the best landlord-tenant relationship is one in which we don't need to talk anymore after this. That means I don't knock on your door (because you pay rent on time), and you don't call me (because no repairs are needed). You got it, Mr. Tenant?" This might sound cold or cruel. But it's the truth, and I would rather have a tenant that's on the same page as me. The more they leave me alone to enjoy my semi-retired life, the better this relationship will be.

Now we are at step 3 of the new landlord to-do list. This is my favorite part of the whole thing! Remember, a penny saved is a penny earned. Every single penny of expenditure you cut from your monthly expenses goes directly into your pocket, so don't be shy. Here are places to look to cut expenses:

1. Utilities such as electric (outdoor or leasing office), water, and gas. Since the utility companies are all monopolies, I can't really negotiate with them. I will simply call them and inform them that I am the new owner and ask if they have any promotion plans. They will usually have some promotions for new accounts, at least for the short term. Take advantage of them!

2. Trash removal. In the city where my property is located, there are two main companies handling trash pickup. I know it's a very profitable business with big margins. So I would get quotes from one company and then use those quotes to leverage the second company for a better price. For all three apartments I have, I saved about 35% with a newly negotiated contract. Not too bad, huh?

3. Landscaping. One of my complexes covers approximately 2 acres of land where weeds and trash are rampant, so weekly groundskeeping is often necessary. I saved about 40% by negotiating a new two-year agreement with the landscaping company. The other thing you can do is turn the lawn into desert landscaping, which can look nice if done correctly. Initially, there are high costs, but you never have to worry about water bills or the sprinkler system breaking down again.

Chapter 6: Starting Out

4. Install water-saving devices such as showerheads, sink faucets, water-saving toilets (which will cost about $150, including installation), motion sensor lights, and new LED lighting. Small savings add up!

5. Close the pool. Yes, pools attract more potential tenants and make the property look attractive, but I estimate the monthly cost to be $200 for pool maintenance & chemicals, another $400 for water bills, $300 for electricity, and $50 for city licensing fees — that's almost a thousand dollars a month just to have a pool! Thanks, but no thanks! On day one of taking over my first apartment complex, I shut down the pool and lost ZERO existing tenants.

6. Because property insurance is a large portion of your monthly expenses, spend some time getting quotes from different agents to get the best deal. The key is to have a higher deductible to save on monthly premiums. I would sign up with basic coverage and avoid filing any claims whatsoever, unless it's something major that would cost more than ten thousand dollars, for example.

7. Negotiate new rates with existing or new vendors: electricians, plumbers, handymen, water heater repairmen, pest control, and appliance repairmen. Handymen typically charge between $15 and $25 an hour. More specialized people such as AC repairmen or plumbers charge more, and the charges usually depend on what they're fixing. I ask my vendors always to call to get my approval before starting any work so that I can understand 1) what the problem is, 2) exactly what they are doing to fix the problem, 3) how long the fix is going to take, and 4) how much they are going to charge me to complete the work. I make it very clear that they must get my prior approval for any work exceeding $200, or they will not be paid. I once worked with a carpenter who did excellent work, but he would show up whenever he wanted and never called ahead of the job to get my approval. I had to let him go. Remember, you are the customer, and contractors must oblige by your rules; if they don't, you'll be better off working with someone else in the long run.

8. Open a company checking account at a local bank within walking distance of the apartment complex. I have already mentioned the reasoning behind this. This way, tenants can deposit the rent at the local bank, and there will be no more excuses about why they cannot pay rent on time. All they have to do is write their apartment number on the bank deposit slip, make the deposit to

your account, and then text the receipt to you along with their apartment number. Nice and easy. This is a million-dollar tip! There will be no more knocking on doors trying to collect rent, no more online payments with the processing company or credit card company taking 2% of the rent, and no more paying apartment management software subscriptions fees. This is the most efficient and cost-saving way to get tenants to pay their monthly rent. I am just surprised at how few landlords use this method!

9. When I buy a property that uses a management company, I always ask the seller to let me come in for a couple of days to work with the existing property manager before the close of escrow. Most sellers agree to my request. I go in and find out the following pertinent information: 1) review the rent roll and learn as much about the tenants as you can (are they late payers? Complainers? Any other issues?); 2) get the contact info of all the vendors they use (repairmen, the company that services the laundry room, etc.); 3) find out if there are any deferred maintenance items on the property or any potential issues with the ac/electric/plumbing systems, etc.; 4) get a list of equipment that belongs to the owner; and 5) walk the property with them to see if there is anything else they can tell you. With this information, you can decide whether you want to keep the property management company on for another couple of months before you let them go. I recommend stipulating at the time of closing that all service contracts terminate with the sale. This gives you the freedom to make the right business decisions once you take over. For one of the properties I bought, the previous owner agreed to let the property management company charge 20% of the net income. That's insane! Once I took over, I kept the management company for five days to learn everything I needed to learn about the property and canceled the agreement with them right after. Property management companies are like vampires that suck up all the profits. Get rid of them as soon as possible!

10. Get rid of any expense you deem unnecessary. The previous owner of one of my properties issued a weekly newsletter and mailed it to all the tenants. He also organized monthly parties that cost $200 per event, and any tenant that paid rent on time could participate in a drawing to win $100 worth of prizes. The previous landlord said this was a good way to promote a sense of community and encourage tenants to pay rent on time. What a bunch of nonsense! He did not understand that people respond better to negative

consequences than rewards. I let all my tenants know that I have zero tolerance for late rent; pay on the 1st, or face eviction. This way, they put the rent invoice on top of their pile of monthly bills instead of the bottom. For that apartment complex, I remember that it was the 8th of the month, and the rent roll showed a rent collection of only 65%. What!? The newsletter and parties were a blatant waste of $300 a month. Once I took over, I immediately canceled both, which saved me roughly $350 a month or $4200 a year! Within three months of implementing my system, I consistently collected over 95% of the rent by the 3rd of every month. Tenants here apparently respond better to the stick than the carrot.

11. Consider turning the laundry room into another unit. Laundry services are convenient for the tenants, but they're also money-losing investments. So I convert all my laundry rooms to either a studio or a one-bedroom apartment when possible. I will share my story below.

When I first got into this business, I had no idea how on-site laundry rooms worked. So I did some research online, and I learned that laundry servicing companies (let's refer to the specific company as ABC Company) provide the washing and drying machines. They come to collect the coins, and then they directly deposit money into my bank account. I did some further research, and the result was shocking to me. If I continued to use their service, after deducting the water and electric bill (which I was paying for), I would lose about $1000 a month! That's 12,000 a year! I absolutely would not continue a contract that cost me so much money a month. That left me with two options: 1) void the contract with ABC and turn the laundry room into my own profit center by putting in my own coin machines, or 2) convert the space into a rentable unit. I did the financial analysis and determined that I could make more money by converting the space into a studio charging $700 per month. I would pay about 35,000 to convert the laundry room to a livable studio, but it would increase my property value by about $85,000. That's a no brainer! Before I could carry out my plan, I had to find a way to void the laundry room contract signed by the previous owner. I was lucky; it turned out their machines broke down all the time, so I knew I might have something there I could use. I read over the agreement carefully and found a termination clause. I wrote them a certified letter telling them about the broken machines and asking them to repair the units within five business days or terminate the agreement. They did not make the repairs, so on the 6th day, I emptied the laundry room. I put all their machines (six washing machines and six dryers) out on the street and locked up the unit. I then wrote them a letter telling them to come to pick up their machines within three business days, or I would charge them storage fees. I knew I was taking a risk that ABC might sue me. According to my lawyer, they would have a 50/50 chance of winning a lawsuit and could ask me to compensate them for the machines and lost revenue. But I also knew that they were a big company, had other fish to fry, and might just let this one slide. It has been three years now. They have written me numerous threatening letters that I don't even bother reading and just toss into the garbage bin. Fingers crossed that hopefully, this is the end of it. Meanwhile, it took me two months to convert the laundry room into a studio, and now I am collecting over $700 a month in rent from this particular unit. Yippy! I have to admit that this was a risky thing to do, and if ABC really came after me for breach of contract, I would have to shell out a lot of money, so I am not suggesting you do this. I am merely sharing what I did that worked. You should consult with your attorney and do what is best for you.

You can also consider turning the management office unit into a studio as well. That would be another $500-700 of income! Yes, you would be losing an office space where you could work and run your business. But I work from home now anyway, and I'm never in the office for longer than 10 minutes when I visit a property. Why waste a potentially profitable space? Instead, turn it into an income-generating resource.

As I have pointed out, every penny I save goes straight into my pocket, and every little bit counts. Aggressively shaving the expenses alone saved me over 20% of monthly costs, and guess what, that money goes straight into my pocket!

After taking over a new apartment, I spend every day at the property for one straight month to continually look for ways to cut costs and identify "troublemakers" amongst my tenants. Who are the troublemakers?

1. Tenants that pay rent late or not at all. Many times, to ensure escrow goes through smoothly, the seller or previous landlord would just rent to anyone,

Chapter 6: Starting Out

even unqualified tenants, just to keep the complex full. Incoming landlords like me sometimes need to clean house when they first take over.

2. Tenants involved in any illegal dealings such as selling drugs.

3. Tenants who cause a mess in their front yard, or worse, damage to the unit.

My philosophy is to deal with problems head-on. I know that people rarely change, so on the 1st of the month following the purchase of a property, I immediately identify who those troublemakers are. When dealing with them, I put my foot down and stay firm. I have heard many excuses for not paying rent on time, including some really crazy ones! One tenant told me her dad (who lived with her) had cancer, and she needed an extension on the rent. I ran into her dad the following day, and he didn't have any idea about any cancer. I gave it some thought; property rental is a business, and I was there to make money. The bank that extended me the loan would not give me a payment extension, so why should I give tenants a rent extension? I was also not there to find out who's telling the truth and who's lying. So I decided to simply enforce the rule 100% of the time from then on. I do not feel guilty about running my business like a business and keeping personal feelings and emotions out of it.

Before I started landlording, I had never been to court. The only court experience I had was watching Judge Judy on TV. But now, going to court for eviction cases is a monthly occurrence for me. I want to share my first court experience with you. One of my tenants had stopped paying rent and was served with a notice to appear in court. He appeared in court dressed in a suit, which I had never seen before since he's a construction worker and always dressed down when I met with him. He also had a pile of pictures and papers in front of him. I knew right away I was in for a fight. Usually, one judge takes care of all the eviction cases, which generally means this is only the type of case he does. That is great news for landlords since he has heard all the excuses out there and tends to rule on the landlord's side. There were 12 cases that morning. Once it was my turn, my attorney and I, along with the defendant, walked up to the judge. The judge asked the tenant why he did not pay rent. The tenant first claimed that he was never served with a 5-day non-payment notice, so I presented the judge with a copy of the notice I had given him personally. The judge sided with me. Then the tenant made several excuses, such as claiming the landlord did not do repairs promptly, which made the unit unlivable, or that he always paid rent late, so there was no reason for the landlord to take him to court this time. But for every excuse he made, the judge would just respond with, "so did you pay rent on time?" This back and forth went on for a full 2 minutes. I was laughing like crazy on the inside because I knew I would win the case (which I did). I didn't even have to open my mouth to speak the whole time, and I won. I learned from this experience to document everything, serve timely notices, present the evidence at court, and speak only when the judge asks me a question. That is the trick of winning eviction court cases.

For drug-using or dealing tenants, just give them a non-renewal notice. You might ask how you can find out who they are. It's actually pretty easy; just talk to the neighbors. As long as you let them know that you will keep their identity confidential, they will be more than willing to tell you who the dealers are. I don't blame them; who wants to live next to a drug dealer? And being the good new landlord that I am, I will get rid of a bad neighbor for them. Win-win.

My philosophy for dealing with troublemaking tenants is, "the longer I keep them around, the more trouble they will cause." If I become an "enabler," it'll seem to other good tenants that I gave them permission to pay rent late or cause trouble on my property. Lo and behold, everyone else will start doing the same. Why not? Since the landlord is such a pushover, let's see how far I can push him. This might sound cruel, but it's the reality of things. So when I see trouble, I hit it head-on and resolve it on the spot. Get rid of the bad apple now, no exceptions.

Since you bought the property, the tenants have now seen you paint the buildings' exterior, make some changes to the landscaping, and even do some repairs inside the units. Now is the perfect time to raise the rent. This needs to be done carefully since you just took over the property, and you don't know how many people will stay and how many will want to leave. The rule of thumb is to pick out the bottom fifth of tenants currently paying the lowest rent and raise their rents first. Let's say my new property has 20 units. I would pick out four units with tenants who are paying rent furthest from the market rates. Most of the tenants are lifelong renters, and they all expect rent to go up when a new owner takes over, so it should not come as a surprise. The goal is to keep as many good tenants as possible, knowing it's cheaper to keep them around than to go out and find new ones. The tricky part is to figure out how much to increase the rent so that it's tolerable for the good tenants. I typically split the difference between the current rent and the market rate. For example, if the current asking rent is $500 and the market rent is $620, I would raise the rent to $560ish. The one exception is if the tenant is a "troublemaker," as I defined earlier. In that case, I would increase their rent to $650 to get them out. Troublemaking tenants give you headaches as long as they stay around, so this is the best opportunity to get rid of them. Instead of giving them a 30-day non-renewal notice, which seems like you are kicking them out, you let them decide to move out since they think the new rent is too high. This works 100% of the time. I have gotten rid of many bad tenants by simply raising their rent. After I raise it, they just leave voluntarily.

The fifth and the last step of the to-do list after taking over a new property is setting up an easy to follow system to make everything automatic. When writing up the protocols, take both money and time into consideration. Keep asking yourself, "what should I do in this situation that will be the most cost-effective, yield me the most profits, and save me the most time?" Also, ask if a particular task is something you can delegate to someone else entirely, so you don't have to be involved at all. There's my formula to set up a 3-step protocol. The first part is to identify the issue I need to resolve. The second part is to figure out what I need to do to resolve the issue as fast as possible. The third part is to think about how I can do better the next time this happens. Keep adjusting and revising rules for the better use of your time. That's the key to a good system.

The top five things to do seems like a lot of work, and it is. One of the complexes I acquired has about 50 units, and I was able to get all five tasks done within two weeks, working 18 hours a day. It's not hard to do, but it is time-consuming for sure. The key to getting everything done quickly is to spend 80% of your time planning and 20% of your time executing and implementing. Also, since you can find anything online nowadays, whenever you need a tenant form, just google it, and you can probably find it easily. Then just customize it for your particular property.

CHAPTER 7
Turning Apartments

"The less inside the unit, the less stress in my head."

That's my motto when deciding how to turn my apartment units. Being a good landlord is simple: provide hot water, heat, air conditioning, and working plumbing for the tenant, and that's about it.

The following is a simple checklist I use when turning my units:

1. Do a quick walkthrough and decide if I need to repaint the units or simply clean the dirt off the walls. If I need to repaint the interior, I use the same Navajo White Semi-Gloss paint color for every unit.

2. If there is carpet, replace it with basic ceramic tiles (which cost 50 cents each). For an 800 square foot unit, that would cost me about $1000, including material and labor.

3. Get rid of all window blinds because they break easily, and get rid of closet doors because they can get loose from their tracks. Finally, get rid of the kitchen garbage disposal because it breaks easily. Remove the shower curtains and the curtain rods they came with. Replace bedroom and bathroom doorknobs with knobs that don't have keyholes or locks. The exterior door should only have a keyed lock on the deadbolt on top; the bottom doorknob should not have locks or keys. These steps will make the unit much easier to manage. Remember, the less that's inside the units, the fewer things a tenant can break, thus reducing the headaches you will have down the road.

4. Check to ensure the heater, air conditioner, stove/oven, electrical plugs, toilets, showerheads, and faucets are working. Flush the toilet and run the water

Chapter 7: Turning Apartments

to ensure it does not get clogged. Check to ensure there is hot water by running the water heater. Install a new air filter for the A/C, which can extend the life of your A/C units. Install new plastic electrical plug plates (which cost 80 cents each) that make the apartments look more recent and updated.

5. Install water-saving AERATORS for kitchen and bathroom faucets to increase water pressure while using less water. 10% of tenants will remove them, and there's nothing you can do about that. But the ones that stay on will save you lots of water, which goes directly to your bottom line.

6. Replace old showerheads with new, water-saving showerheads (which cost about $10 if you buy them in bulk). Install a water-saving device in the toilet or replace the old toilet with a new water-saving toilet. Altogether, this will cost you around $200, including labor, but it's well worth it! Replace any toilets that are 15 years or older or have 5-gallon flushes with newer models that flush just 1.5 gallons instead. Then install a toilet water saver so it'll flush even less water each time. This tip alone will save you thousands per year, which goes straight into your pocket! Remember, most of the water is master metered and is the landlord's responsibility, so you want to be extra careful to cut down on as many water-related expenses as possible.

7. Remove window screens, window exhaust fans, toilet paper holders, towel bars in the bathroom, ceiling fans, and any unnecessary light fixtures. Also, get rid of the refrigerator. You might question this move, so let me explain my logic behind this. First, check with your state's housing laws; my state does not require the landlord to provide a refrigerator. The problem with refrigerators is that they can break easily if the tenant does not use them properly. Many tenants shop at places like Costco and overfill their fridge, which causes the airways inside to get blocked. Eventually, the refrigerator will stop working altogether. Most of the time, it's much cheaper just to buy a used fridge than to repair the existing one (which costs about $120 to $150, including delivery). I used to have so many refrigerators breaking down that I decided to let all the new incoming tenants buy their own fridges when they moved in. Most of them get upset when I explain that I don't provide a refrigerator and they have to purchase their own, but once I tell them that they can buy one cheaply for around $120, they are ok with it. I give them the contact information for the people I used to purchase the fridges from. Because it is their fridge, they are

responsible for repairs or replacement if it breaks down during their tenancy. Imagine the number of headaches I saved myself by not having to deal with countless refrigerator issues!

8. Cabinets are probably the most expensive item if they require replacement, and replacement parts can be challenging to find. I recommend removing the cabinet handles and having a groove cut out at the bottom of the cabinet doors so tenants can slide their fingers underneath to open them. The cabinet panels are expensive to replace, so repaint them as much as you can. The worst-case scenario is when a drawer's door becomes loose, and the tenant just rips it off and throws it away. It'll be impossible to find a replacement. Usually, I'll just have my handyman cut out a piece of wood, paint it the same or similar color, and then just nail it up to cover up the space. Yes, the tenant loses some storage space, but I always make sure there are plenty of other storage areas available.

9. Use the same paint colors, light fixtures, faucet types, showerheads, water saver devices, etc., throughout the units. Purchase plenty of supplies and inventory when it goes on sale at home improvements stores, or better yet, buy them in bulk on Amazon to get an even bigger discount.

10. Keep the big trees since their roots have usually extended deep enough to be fed by underground water, so they don't need any watering. Eliminate as many bushes, shrubs, and grasses as possible, and instead use desert landscaping. The water bill is one of the largest expenses, so try to find creative ways to lower this expense as much as possible.

11. Leave windows alone if there's nothing wrong with them. I was lucky enough to have a reliable window guy who charges me $50 to repair a window, and he does it in 10 minutes. When there's a broken window, I just tell the tenant to pay for it in advance, and I usually charge them $80, so they pay for my time as well.

12. When the water heater leaks, just replace it. Used water heaters are $200 each, and brand new ones are $500+. Other kinds of water heater repair usually cost about $80.

Chapter 7: Turning Apartments

13. Once you have finished turning the unit and it's ready for showing, have other tenants keep their eyes on it. Squatters or previous tenants sometimes break in and just start living there. I have recently evicted a tenant for non-payment, and she left the place in a big mess with tons of damages, so it took me about two weeks to get it ready for showing. The night I finished turning the unit, she broke the back window and snuck back in, and spent the night sleeping on the floor. My helper saw her the following morning and told me. I called the cops and had her arrested for trespassing. Apparently, she had been sleeping in a nearby park after she was evicted. Once the unit was ready for rent, her ex-neighbor (who was a friend of hers) told her about it, and she just snuck back in. I gave her friend a notice of non-renewal immediately. The other reason you want to tell other tenants about vacancies is so they can tell their friends. Half of my new tenants were referred by their friends, who are existing tenants. They obviously like living here and are used to how I manage this property, so they refer their friends to me, and I don't even have to pay them a referral fee! The other good thing is that it minimizes the vacancy time, so I can usually get the place rented within a week of having the unit ready.

Set aside some money for A/C and roof replacement. A used AC unit, including installation, is $2000, and the roof will cost about 8k to 15k for 1500 square feet. For class C apartments especially, you can expect to repair the roof or AC once every three months if you are lucky, so you might as well calculate that into your monthly repair budget.

While stripping the units down to bare bones might sound cruel and make me look like a slumlord, I think it actually makes me a better landlord to the tenants. The less time I spend repairing "extra items," the more time and money I can spend on maintaining essential items, such as fixing the A/C immediately in 100-degree heat or getting the tenant's plumbing issue resolved so they have water. It all depends on how you look at things.

From a business owners' perspective, this is a business and also a livelihood. Some people might think the way I run my business sounds cold and heartless, but I am not here to make friends. Instead, I am here to run a profitable business and put food on the table for my family. I can be a nice guy or sucker, or I can man-up and run it like a business. Given a choice, I choose the latter!

CHAPTER 8
Marketing & Qualifying

"Marketing is simply getting the word out."

In the apartment rental business, as in any business, getting the word out is crucial. This section will cover what types of marketing I have found to be the most efficient and effective. It's all about marketing to potential renters who have the qualifications and money to move in as soon as possible, thus minimizing the number of vacancies.

Whenever I have vacancies, I advertise in Facebook groups and Craigslist. They are both free, and I have found them to be the most effective way to reach the people I am targeting. The best time to advertise is Thursday and Friday at 1 pm and 3 pm and all day Saturday and Sunday. That's when people are either taking a break from work or searching online for a new apartment. I have a template that I use for the posting, along with pictures of the apartment units. Photos are taken using my iPhone and include images of the kitchen, bathroom, living room, bedroom, and the building's exterior showing the landscaping and surrounding areas. There are other useful sites like zillow.com or apartments.com, but I have found that I reach more potential tenants just using Facebook and Craigslist, so I stick with those. To find the best Facebook groups to join, try searching for the term "buy and sell in (name of your city)." Since many of my tenants are Latinos, I post in Spanish groups as well; in that case, you would want to search for groups using terms like "renta" and "venta."

As for the ad itself, keep the headline simple. I usually write something like "1 Bedroom next to Airport $850," then upload the apartment pictures and copy and paste in the description.

Below is a sample description I use:

Chapter 8: Marketing and Qualifying

***** Jefferson 24th Apartment, near Airport, 1 Bedroom $850 *****

Lowest Priced In Town!

One Bedroom: $850 (Available now)

You pay Electric and Gas
Refundable security Deposit $850 - $1200 (depend on your income/rental history/background check)

ONLY ONE LEFT, TEXT US NOW! (555)555-1234

- Address: 1234 N. Jefferson Blvd, Airport City, IN 85512
- Major cross street: Jefferson / 24th Street

- Water, sewer, trash, tax included. You only pay for electricity and gas.
- Cold A/C, stove included.
- Quiet, lots of Parking
- Minutes to the freeway, school, parks, shops, retail, bus, railway
- Move-in ready, Most affordable (10% below market)

If interested, please text me if you meet the following STRICT requirements:

1) Your income needs to be more than $2500 per month.

2) No eviction/judgment/collections, strict income and ex-landlord verification

3) No pets

4) You need to drive by the property before setting up a viewing appointment

- Non-refundable Application Fee of $35 to check your background.

"Landlord does not discriminate based on race, color, religion, national origin, sex, handicap, or familial status."

Millionaire Landlord Secrets

*****Jefferson 24th Apartment*****
www.Jefferson24Apartments.com
(555)555-1234 TEXT NOW to schedule a viewing

    This template has been modified at least 20 times, and everything in the description has a purpose. Let's go over this posting line by line. First, the posting's purpose is to get potential tenants to text me about their interest in the apartment. I want them to text, not call. I use this nice little app called "TextNow," which charges $5 a month for unlimited usage. I get to call and text anyone in the US, and people can call and text me as well. However, I do not take any incoming calls unless I recognize the phone number. Once again, I want potential renters to text me at this number so I can ensure they are qualified and start eliminating the renters I do not want. Even though the posting asks them to text me, some keep calling and never leave a message. This is Elimination #1; I do not want to rent to people who either do not or cannot follow instructions. Besides, I prefer to communicate with tenants via text, so if they do not know how to text, they are just wasting my time. Yes, it might cost me some good tenants, but I think the upsides outweigh the downsides. Some renters call and leave long messages telling me sob stories about how they're victims of abuse and are currently living on the street. They ask me to "do them a favor" by letting them move in. I ignore those calls as well. That's Elimination #2. The third type of call I often get is when prospective renters leave me a message asking that I call them back. What's happening here is that they most likely do not meet all the requirements, so they want to talk to me over the phone to explain themselves. I have no time for that. My time is precious, and I have other fish to fry, so no return calls for those as well. Elimination #3. I just filtered out 50% of the non-qualified renters by simply implementing a "Text and No Call" posting — that alone saves me tons of time!

    My asking rent is $850, and I also ask for an $850 to $1200 security deposit. That amount is actually high in my state. Every state is different, but landlords in my state usually charge half to a full month of rent for the security deposit. To get good tenants, you must ask for a high to very high security deposit and set the rent slightly lower than the market rate. I'll go over the reasons why in a later chapter. I sometimes get calls from renters asking me to work with them

Chapter 8: Marketing and Qualifying

on rent and deposits. Elimination #4. You can now see that everything I put in the posting serves to eliminate as many non-qualified people as possible, so I don't waste my time. I do not even bother to return their calls.

The renters' combined income should be three times the rent. The rule of thumb is that a third of their income is for food, a third is for utilities and miscellaneous items, and a third is for rent. The next item in our ad is "no evictions, judgments, or felonies." Even if they had an eviction 20 years ago, I would turn them away. The eviction process has many steps, and if they don't pay rent and still go through the steps and drag the landlord into the mud along the way, that's malicious. I don't even want to deal with this type of person or consider whether they have changed and are now a better renter. Elimination #5.

As I mentioned before, I have a strict no pet or animal policy in my units. Elimination #6. As for renters claiming they have service animals, make sure they have legitimate paperwork showing that their animals are indeed service animals, not just a "doctor's note." 90% of the "proof" I have received is bogus, so watch out for that. Ask them to text you the proof so you can verify it before showing them the apartment.

I ask all potential renters to drive by the neighborhood before making an appointment with me. Yes, this is a hassle for the renter, having to drive to the property twice before viewing the unit, but it saves me time. Some renters are also new to the area and have no clue about the different neighborhoods. I have no time to spend with them on the phone explaining what type of neighborhood this complex is in and so on. Elimination #7.

The non-refundable application fee of $35 does two things. First, it filters out the renters that tried to submit applications to multiple complexes since they are most likely not qualified renters. Second, it pays me for my time. Each application will take at least 30 minutes to an hour of my time to review, and I need to get paid as well. Elimination #8.

I end the posting with non-discrimination statements and my phone number so prospective renters can text me to express their interest. As you can see, this short posting has all the information a potential renter needs, and it filters out 80% of the non-qualified renters for me. Now that's a win-win!

Say that a renter has texted me and told me that he or she is interested in renting the apartment. The next step is for me to send them a text confirming again they are eligible renters. This is what I text them:

*****Jefferson 24th Apartment***** (available NOW!)
One Bedroom: $850

You pay APS electric

Refundable security deposit $850 - $1200
Major Cross Street is Jefferson and 24th St.

We have the following strict requirements:
1) Your income needs to be more than $2500 per month (Include SSI, disabilities, child support, food stamp; Exclude Unemployment)

2) No eviction/judgment/collections, Strict income, and ex-landlord verification

3) No pets

4) You need to drive by the property before setting up a viewing appointment

Do you meet those strict requirements?

If they reply "Yes," I text them my second sets of scripts:

If you meet our strict requirements,
Please call and text Jennifer (555) 555-4321 to schedule a viewing

** Jefferson 24th Apartments **
Address: 1234 N. Jefferson Blvd, Airport City, IN 85512
Major cross street: Jefferson / 24th Street

Chapter 8: Marketing and Qualifying

Please bring $35 for the application fee, your ID, social security card, and three months of pay stubs or bank statements if self-employed.

My name is Jason. Let me know if you can't reach her. Thanks.

You can see here that I give them my helper Jennifer's phone number so the renter can call her directly to arrange a viewing. I will go over how the "helper system" works in a later chapter. I want to point out here that I am asking potential renters to prove that they are serious by 1) taking action by driving by the complex before setting up a viewing and 2) contacting my helpers to arrange a viewing. From a psychological perspective, the more time someone spends on a particular task, in this case, renting an apartment, the more likely they will proceed.

While texting back and forth with prospective tenants, the same thing always happens. When I text my requirements, some people reply with a straight yes or no. If they respond yes, I text them the follow-up script to contact my helper and arrange for a showing. Others want to call me to explain why they don't fit all of my requirements. I have heard all the stories; how sick a person is and why they need a place now, how someone's family is homeless, or excuses for why they've had three evictions in the past two years. I have no time for their sob stories/excuses/dramas; it's just a complete waste of my time. I ignore them and move on to the next potential leads. This might sound cold, but 99% of the time, their explanations are lame excuses or straight-up lies. Also, my time is expensive and precious. I have no time to listen to their stories and figure out if they are telling the truth or lying. Either way, I know I am better off not even responding to them and spending my time finding other, more qualified tenants.

I want to mention a couple of additional pointers here as well. One of my complexes is located a three-minute walk from an elementary school. Whenever I have vacancies, I put flyers on the windshields of cars in the school parking lot. Those are the best renters since it is almost guaranteed that those families will not move for at least six years while their kids are in school. I seldom have trouble filling out vacancies in this particular complex. Because I know that this complex's location and proximity to the local school is a huge selling point, I use the phrase "close to XXX school" in my headline when I advertise.

It usually takes me about a week to turn a unit after a tenant has moved out, assuming they did not cause any significant damage during their tenancy. At the beginning of my landlording career, I would try to "pre-market," meaning I would try to start advertising while still turning the unit. That is just a complete waste of time. I would set up a viewing appointment a week away, and by the time the unit was ready for viewing, they would have already found another place. The goal is to spend the least amount of time filling vacancies; "pre-marketing" is just not a very good use of time.

I placed prominent real estate signage out in front of the complex that is noticeable to people driving or walking by. These people know the area well, and because the complex is convenient to their school or work, they will most likely be long term tenants. I have recently been getting many new tenants referred by existing tenants in the complex. This makes the whole process so much easier because those new renters already know what the apartments look like since they have seen their friends' or family's units. Thus, I do not have to do any showings. They also know my management style because their friends and families have told them. There will be no surprises. Of course, I still have to review their applications to ensure they meet all the qualifications. But if everything goes well, I prefer to rent to them since chances are, they will be long-term tenants.

I have encountered a common scam that I want to mention here, so you are forewarned. One day, I got a call out of the blue from a lady asking me for the keys to move in. I had no idea who she was, and as far as I knew, my helper had just started showing the unit the day before and had not received any applications. Apparently, she saw another ad similar to mine that some guy posted on Craigslist. The guy arranged the showing with my helper and then pretended to be the landlord when the woman arrived. He also made her an excellent offer, stating if she paid the monthly rent of $500 in cash that day (which is way below my asking rent of $850), he would waive the deposit. With such a good deal, of course, she accepted. She paid the guy cash on the spot without signing any lease or getting any receipt and then showed up at the door asking for the keys to move in. I had to go over and explain to her that she was

Chapter 8: Marketing and Qualifying

scammed and there was nothing we could do to help her. I asked her to contact the police instead. It sounds like a crazy story, but it happened to me. If you stick with landlording long enough, you will see everything! Remember never to share specific unit numbers in your advertisements to avoid squatters breaking into the units. Now let's move on to the next chapter, where I will go into pricing and marketing in more detail.

Below are the steps my helper follows when showing the unit:

1. Check the unit 15 mins before the appointment time to ensure it's presentable. Remember, the unit may have been sitting vacant for a while now and might be stuffy inside. My helper sweeps up any dirt and opens all the windows and doors to ensure good air circulation.

2. When the prospective tenants arrive, introduce the apartment, pointing out that it's quiet, close to stores and freeways, etc. Answer any questions the potential renters have.

3. Take note of the applicant's vehicle, attitudes, punctuality, and appearance.

4. Ask questions and let them talk! You want to find out as much about this renter as possible.

5. Get the renters to fill out an application on the spot. My helper collects the $35 application fee, of which they get to keep $25.

6. Take pictures of the completed application, renter's IDs, and last three months of their pay stubs. My helper then texts everything to me.

CHAPTER 9
Pricing and Positioning

"To best position yourself to succeed, know your competitors."

When I first started, I met an experienced landlord through a mutual friend. He was about my age and a very bright guy who owned about 80 single-family homes. He gave me a ton of good advice. One of the things he told me was that he always charged rent a little less than the market rate to keep his units full. It's better to charge a little less per unit than to have units sit empty for a whole month. Setting the asking rent to be a little below the market rate makes it easier to fill the vacancy. Also, existing tenants know the market rate, so they know they are getting a good deal and will want to stick around longer. Thus, you create a good cycle where you keep your units full all the time.

It is critical to keep an eye on the market rate. I know my price needs to be competitive; it's important to balance maximizing profits and minimizing the number of vacancies and headaches. What I do is keep a list of all my competitors within a 2-mile radius. I call them every three months to find out what they are asking for their units. I would like to call more often, even once a month, but I don't want them to recognize my voice. Then I adjust my prices to 5-10% less than what my competitors are asking. If my vacancies are below 4% or if I get overwhelming responses to my Craigslist or Facebook group postings, then I know my asking rent is too low. I will then keep raising rent until I hit a plateau where either my vacancy rate is higher than 4% or I am not getting as many calls.

In a soft market, when the economy is not doing well and people are losing their jobs, it is better to lower the asking rent strategically. However, never lower the security deposit; if anything, raise the deposit to attract better tenants. Good paying tenants tend to pay rent on time. They are also less likely to

Chapter 8: Marketing and Qualifying

damage the property, so they typically don't mind paying a higher security deposit since they know they will get it back when they leave the unit. Never be afraid to ask for higher deposits. I am actually considering asking for a 1.5-month security deposit now. High deposits will encourage the tenants to return the unit in a clean and undamaged condition to get their money back.

When reviewing applications, I do not discriminate based on race, sex, religion, or age. Having said that, I also know what type of tenants tend to stay long-term. It's essential to have a niche area to focus on in any business so you can target a particular market segment and advertise to them. Like any landlord, I prefer to rent to long-term tenants. I have found that they are usually between 35-60 years old, have stable jobs and no criminal history, have incomes between $2000-3000 a month, and are either younger couples with families or single older adults living alone. Most renters in this particular demographic will stay for the long haul. Because turnover is the single most costly expense a landlord has, if I have multiple applications for the same unit, I will choose the ones I think are most suitable for the complex and who will stick around the longest. Once you have identified the market segment ideal for your business, you can correctly position your business/apartment building to ensure continued success.

Once your units are full, you can pull down all the postings and stop returning text messages or Facebook messages. There is just no point in leaving them active. When I first started, I tried to save potential renters' phone numbers, thinking I could call them back when I had vacancies the following week. Unfortunately, it just doesn't work that way. It's also not a very good use of time. It is more efficient to turn the units first, get them ready to show, and then advertise and market them. Work smarter, not harder.

CHAPTER 10
Qualifying & Leasing

"To avoid headaches and bad tenants, stop them from coming in in the first place."

Now the renters have viewed the apartment with your helper. Say that one person, in particular, liked the unit and submitted an application to your helper along with his ID and last three-months of paystubs. Next, your helper took pictures of all those documents and texted them to you via the TextNow app. Now it's your turn to review the applications. This is a crucial task, if not the single most vital part of landlording, so I will spend about a quarter of this book explaining how to identify good renters. Hang in there; I guarantee you will find this chapter very useful to your landlording career!

When reviewing tenant applications, I put myself in a mindset I call "defensive landlording," in which I question and scrutinize everything on the application. I verify every piece of information. If the tenant left something blank on the application for some reason, I always assume the worst: they have something to hide. Some people might call me paranoid, and they are right! This is my business and my livelihood; I am renting to a complete stranger that I know nothing about who could potentially harm my business! If people knew the ordeals I went through because I let the wrong people into my apartments, they wouldn't be calling me paranoid; instead, they would call me smart! When dealing with renters on the phone, I am not shy about asking any questions. I ask them to tell me about their past criminal history if I see a need, for example. Sometimes they get offended, but I don't care. I am here to protect my business, and if they don't want to answer my questions or address my concerns, no problem, they can just look elsewhere to live.

The following is a rental application that I use for potential renters:

Chapter 10: Qualifying and Leasing

Date: _____ Address Applying for: _____ # of Bedroom: ____ Last Name: _____

RENTAL APPLICATION $35.00 (Non-Refundable, Each Adult MUST Apply)

ONLY CLEAN & RESPONSIBLE PEOPLE WHO PAY RENT ON TIME MAY APPLY with valid Picture ID

Full Name:	SSN#	Date of Birth:
Cell Phone:	Email:	

List Your Addresses for the Previous 5 Years

Current Address:	City, State, Zip:	
Owner/Manager:	Phone:	Monthly Rent:
Moved in date:	Why are you moving:	
Previous Address:	City, State, Zip:	
Owner/Manager:	Phone:	Monthly Rent:
Moved in date:	Moved out date:	Why:
Previous Address:	City, State, Zip:	
Owner/Manager:	Phone:	Monthly Rent:
Moved in date:	Moved out date:	Why:

Employment and Income

Current Employer:	Address:	
Position:	Phone:	Hire Date:	Hours worked per week:
Gross Wages $	(__ month __ week __ hour)	Other Income (SSI, Disability, Food Stamp, Child Support): $
Supervisor's Name:	Supervisor's Phone:	
Are You on Section 8:	If Yes, How much are you approved for: $	Please provide your voucher & paperwork
How Long Will You Live Here: __ 1 yr __ 2 yr __ 3 yr +	Your Attorney's Name:	
How much do you have for move in now?	Have You Broken A Lease:	Have You Ever Had Bed Bugs:
How many felony or misdemeanor do you have?	What kind of animals do you have:	Weight:
How Many Evictions Have Been Filed On You:	What may interrupt your income or ability to pay rent:	

If Accepted The Following People Will Be Living in My Household

1.) Name:	DOB:	4.) Name:	DOB:
2.) Name:	DOB:	5.) Name:	DOB:
3.) Name:	DOB:	6.) Name:	DOB:

Do You Have A Checking Account:	Balance:
Do You Have a Savings Account:	Balance:

There is a $100 fee if rent is not paid on or before 1st of the month, plus $10 per day. There is no Grace Period. Do you Agree?

EMERGENCY CONTACTS Including Help To Pay Rent

NAME	ADDRESS	PHONE	RELATIONSHIP
1.)			
2.)			

LIST All Vehicles & Trailers of your household: _____
How did you find this apartment: (friend, facebook, craigslist, google, yard sign, etc.) _____

Your Requested Move-In Date: _____ How Much Cash Do You Have: $ _____ Next Page ->

As a rule of thumb, I aim to spend approximately 30-40 minutes reviewing each application. Whenever my gut tells me they are lying about something, I end the phone interview and reject their application altogether. My philosophy is that I would much rather have a unit sitting empty than have someone move in and immediately cause trouble or stop paying rent. It takes at least 1-2 months to go through the eviction process, not to mention countless hours of losing sleep. It's just not worth it!

The first step of the reviewing process is to make sure you have all the information in front of you. You will need the applicant's ID (driver's license and social security card), the last three months of their paycheck stubs from their current employer, and the application. All those documents should have been texted to you when they submitted their application. Before calling the applicant, always call their employer and current landlord. This can get tricky because you're calling phone numbers provided by the applicant, but there are ways to outsmart them if they happen to be lying. First, look at their paycheck stub to ensure it is from the last three months. I have had people send me year old papers hoping that I wouldn't look! Second, google the company's name to see if it's legitimate and determine their phone number. Instead of calling the phone number listed on the application, call the company's main line and ask the receptionist if they have so and so working there. Most of the time, the receptionist will verify that the applicant works there. Then ask the receptionist for the applicant's direct supervisor. Once you get a hold of the employer, identify yourself as the property manager wanting to do employment verification for his staff. Ask questions like, "Is so and so working for you? For how long? Is he a reliable worker? How many hours does he work per week? Do you expect to keep him on?" Most of the time, the employer will answer your questions over the phone, even if he is limited in what he can say due to privacy laws. If you don't ask for too many details, you should have no problem getting your questions answered on the spot. Sometimes, on rare occasions, the employer refers me to their Human Resources Department. If that happens to you, say something like this, "Sir, I will do that. Just one last quick question for you, do you feel the applicant is a good reliable worker?" Notice, you are asking him how he "feels" about the applicant. Nine and out of ten people I have asked this question to don't mind giving me a quick yes or no answer, and that's all I need. Suppose the employer hesitates before answering your question. In that case, you can assume the worst, that the applicant either does not work there or is not a good worker and thus won't be employed there much longer. Also, the Human Resources Department usually requires me to fax them a formal request with my company letterhead on top. That's just a lot of hassle that I avoid doing. I believe talking to the applicant's direct supervisor and trying to get as much out of him as possible is the best way to go.

It gets even trickier when trying to verify the applicant's current landlord. Keep in mind that 50% of the time, I am given either a bogus phone number or a number belonging to the applicant's friends or family. Always google the address provided by the applicant and see whether it's a legitimate address, and then do a "bird-eye" view on google to see what it looks like. If it's a big apartment complex, simply Google the phone number and cross-check it with the phone number on the application. If it matches, that's a good sign that tells you the applicant isn't afraid that you'll call their existing landlord. Usually, this means he's already given them notice or is leaving on good terms. Afterward, call the apartment complex and ask the receptionist for the name of the property manager the applicant listed on his application. Say something like this, "Hi. I am calling from Jefferson 24 Apartments to do a residence verification for Mr. Jones. Can you please tell me if he is a good tenant and if he has already given you a notice that he'll be moving out?" Half the time I ask this question, I get a straight answer over the phone. The other half of the time, they ask me to fax them a signed verification form. Once again, you want to be efficient and get a quick answer, so say, "Sure, I'll get that faxed over as soon as possible, but one last quick question for you. Knowing what you know now, would you rent to Mr. Jones again?" Once again, you are giving her a chance to provide a quick yes or no answer. So far, I have not had any current landlord refuse to answer that question for me. Trust me; if the applicant is a tenant from hell, the current landlord knows his name by heart and will respond without hesitation. If Google Maps shows a house, you will have to rely on the phone number provided by the applicant. Call the number and ask, "Hi, do you have a two-bedroom for rent?" Whoever answers should not hesitate to give a quick yes or no answer. If the answer is an immediate yes, that confirms the person you are speaking with is most likely a real landlord, not the applicant's friend or family. You can then continue with your questions, "So how many bedrooms did he rent from you, how much rent did he pay, and was he a good tenant?" All those questions should have quick answers too.

If the answer is a firm no, that means this family member or friend forgot to lie on the applicant's behalf, and you have just exposed the applicant's lies.

In some cases, I can't obtain verification from previous landlords, either because they're concerned about the legal liability or because they don't want to lose a good tenant. I then call the potential renter and ask, "Mr. Renter, as you know, we do very strict background checks when reviewing new tenant applications. I could not get a good reference from your previous landlord, so why don't you be honest and tell me what's going on? Are you leaving on bad terms or getting evicted?" This straightforward type of questioning forces the applicant to tell you the trust most of the time. I have found it to be very effective.

I learned about the application verification steps above after making hundreds, if not thousands, of calls. If you follow the instructions above, you will get verification within 5 to 7 minutes tops. It is so important to do everything in the most efficient and time-saving way possible. And remember, any hesitation in the answers should raise doubt; you will learn this after making about ten or so calls.

Deciding to accept or reject an application is not difficult and should not take more than 30 minutes of your time. After those two calls, I will decide whether to reject the application now or continue to the next step, calling the applicant himself.

When calling the applicant on the phone, I have a list of prepared questions to ask. The reason for the call is to filter out potentially bad tenants who have most likely been evicted multiple times and jump from available space to space. Such tenants are trying to trick the landlord into believing in their lies, immediately stop paying rent after moving in, and live there rent-free for as long as possible. Sometimes I will ask the same question twice to catch prospective tenants in their own lies. Just like Judge Judy says, "You don't need to have a good memory if you just tell the truth." Below I will list the questions I ask renters when I call them and explain why each is important and what I do with their answers. Remember, I am doing the final qualification when going through my list with them on the phone. Anytime I don't hear the "right answer," or my gut tells me they are lying, I politely end the call and reject their

Chapter 10: Qualifying and Leasing

application — no need to waste another second of my time. Keep in mind that your goal is to find good long-term tenants, so you want to reject as many renters as possible. This line of questioning, or "interrogation," is not easy, but it is very effective in smoking out renters who will not be good fits.

1. "Where do you live now?" Verify their answer against the address they have on their driver's license and application.

2. "How did you hear about us?" This is for my own marketing purposes to know which one of my marketing methods are working.

3. "When do you want to move in?" If they want to move in more than two weeks after submitting their application, I ask them to please call back in two weeks. There is no way I will hold the unit for longer than two weeks. That's half a month's rent!

4. "How much is your monthly income, including food stamps, disability, child support, and SSI"? If the total is less than three times the asking rent, I reject their application.

5. Before I call the applicants, I first go to our county's court website to see if they have any old or pending court cases. The service is free, and the information is updated frequently. I simply put in their first and last name and their date of birth, and then the court website gives me a list of cases under those names. If I see the applicant has an eviction case, I reject their application outright, even if it's from 20 years ago. Sometimes I get applicants with common names like "Alex Jones." In those cases, I call the applicant and rephrase the question by saying something like, "We did a background check and found you have some cases with the court. Please tell me about them." Then I'll just shut up and listen to their answers. If they hesitate before saying it's not them, they are lying, and I reject them outright. If those cases do not pertain to them, they should answer my question firmly and immediately state that it's a mistake and that they have never had a run-in with the law. This is the most important part of the phone interview; it can make the difference between having a good tenant or a 3-month headache. In some cases, the applicant has traffic tickets, some unpaid debt from years ago, or drug possession charges from when they were in high school. I still consider their

application in these cases as long as they are honest when I ask them about it. I also let them know that I will need to charge them a higher security deposit if I approve their applications. Most of them are ok with that. I have found that people with some minor criminal history appreciate the second chance I am giving them and usually turn out to be great tenants. Most of them stay long-term with me, as well. I believe in giving people second chances, just not when they have any eviction history.

6. "What kind of pets do you have?" I ask this question even if they put down that they have no pets or animals. The way I phrase the question assumes that they have a pet already, but if they don't, they should answer my question quickly with a firm No.

7. "How many people will move in with you?" No more than two people per bedroom. Remember, you are paying for water, sewer, and trash, plus wear and tear on the rooms, which will cost you money if more people live there.

8. "The rent is always due by the 1st of the month. Will you be able to pay the rent on the 1st?" Once you ask this question, SAL (shut up and listen) carefully. The answer should be a firm "yes." Then follow up with, "We are very strict about tenants paying rent on time. We have no grace period, and late fees and notice fees will be $100 plus $10 per day starting at 5:01 pm on the 1st of the month, followed by eviction. Are you ok with that?" Their answer should be another firm "yes." All potential renters must understand that you expect them to pay rent on time BEFORE they move in. Do everything you can to impress upon them that you have zero tolerance for any late rent payments.

9. "Did you drive by our property?" If they say no, I ask them to drive by and then text me back to schedule an interior viewing. The purpose of this is not to waste their time, but to save my time.

10. "Why do you want to live here?" If they answer that they want to be closer to work, or that their children are in this school district, or their ex who has custody of their kids lives nearby, Bingo! Those renters will most likely stay longer.

Chapter 10: Qualifying and Leasing

11. "Do you have any questions for me?" This is a good question to ask to determine what the potential renter is looking for and what their concerns are. Below is a list of typical questions I get asked and my responses.

a) "Do you have a washer and dryer inside the unit?" No, is that what you are looking for?

b) "Does the landlord pay for electricity?" No, you pay electricity, which is about $200 a month. Do you have enough income to cover that?

c) "I get paid on the 3rd of the month. Can you work with me on rent?" No, rent is always due by the first of the month. Will you be able to pay the monthly rent on time? Here you can decide if you want to work with them or not. Many renters live off of fixed income like SSI and get paid on the 3rd of the month.

d) "Can you reduce the amount of the deposit?" This is a red flag. The mere fact they're asking this question tells me that they 1) don't make enough money to live here, or 2) might damage the apartment during their tenancy because they don't expect to get their deposit back.

e) "Is there a pool?" No, there is no pool. Is that what you are looking for?

f) "Can I do a month-to-month lease instead of a 12-month lease?" Big Red Flag! They are looking for a short-term motel. In many cases, renters have sold their existing home and are waiting for their new home to close. They want a place to stay temporarily before they can move into their new home and staying at the complex is way cheaper and more comfortable than staying in a motel. So watch out for that.

g) "Can my husband not be on the lease?" No, all adults need to be on the lease. Try to find out why she doesn't want her husband to be on the lease; the answer might surprise you.

h) "Can I paint the place the color I like?" The answer is a big NO. They are most likely first-time renters and are clueless. Be careful when renting to a first-time renter since most of them don't know all the rules and expect Ritz Charlton 5-star service.

i) "Can you do me a big favor and let me move in now without the full amount? I promise to pay you the difference within ten days after moving in" My answer to this question is always a big no. Everyone needs to pay the full amount before moving in, and the fact they're asking me to do them "a favor" now scares me. I reject their application on the spot.

j) "I know you only have a one-bedroom right now. Can I move into the one-bedroom now and switch to a two-bedroom when it becomes available?" The answer is no. I will not go out of my way to accommodate requests like this. Always make sure your unit has the most important feature that a particular renter is looking for. If it doesn't, they'll just be another short-term tenant.

k) "Do you do credit checks?" Even though I don't usually pull their credit report, I still tell them that I do. This ensures they will be honest with me and tell me everything I need to know since they think I'll find out anyway. Many landlords do credit checks. It's not that I care about paying the $25 for the reports; I just don't get any useful information from them. I can get everything I need to know from the local court website. And good credit scores don't guarantee that they will be good tenants. So I don't put too much weight on credit scores, relying instead on my preset line of questions to make my decision.

I saved the best story for last. If you ever hear a renter asking you the following question, hang up the phone! Here is the question: "Can I move in tomorrow? I can even pay you more deposit if you let me move in today. Or I can even clean/turn the apartment for you if you let me move in this afternoon." Big Big Red Flag. They are most likely getting evicted, and they are paying you with the previous landlord's money. And you have to wonder, why would anyone be so desperate that they are willing to pay you a higher deposit and do the cleaning for you? It just doesn't make sense. As Judge Judy says, "When it does not make sense, it's not true." So if a potential tenant asks me the above question, I reject their application on the spot. I have learned this lesson the hard way. I once rented to an applicant who was willing to turn and clean the unit for me because "he couldn't wait to move into a new apartment because his kids were starting school soon." He seemed like a decent family guy, and I was busy, so I did not thoroughly vet him before letting him move

Chapter 10: Qualifying and Leasing

in. Biggest mistake of my life! He stopped paying rent the following month, and he changed the locks and taped up the windows with newspaper so I could not see inside. He refused to answer the door and did not take my calls. I had to start the eviction process just a month after he moved in, and then he made up all sorts of excuses to postpone the eviction hearing. He knew the system well. All in all, it took me 2.5 months to get rid of him when the average eviction time is about three weeks. To top it off, he left the unit in such terrible condition that it cost me another $2500 to repair and clean everything on top of the $500 I had already paid for the eviction. He had put multiple holes in the wall, and there was a smell of dog pee in the bedroom. The cabinets were sprayed with graffiti. He put superglue in all the keyholes, and he even poured cement down the toilet and kitchen sink so that I had to replace the whole sewer pipe. The worst part was that the unit was down for a total of 5 months before I could get it ready. Including the loss in rent and all the fees, this added up to an $8000 mistake, one I will never forget! I later found out that he had had five evictions in the past six years. He's essentially a "habitual squatter." It is unfortunate that we have people like this in society, but this mistake was on me. I take full responsibility since I was the one who did not do my due diligence and allowed him to come in and harm my business. This happened the second year after I started my rental business. Since then, I have always done my homework when reviewing applications! Maybe I should thank him for this costly lesson; after all, it taught me never to be lazy again.

There are a few other things to look for when talking to prospective tenants on the phone. I learned this next lesson from my Psychology class at University (I am actually using something I learned in school, Yippie!) When a renter is talking a lot and talking very fast, they are trying to get one over on you. Turn them down. When a renter gets defensive with your questions, and either gets an attitude or argues with you, reject their application. The key is to ask open-ended questions like, "So tell me about the place you are living right now and why you want to leave," and just listen. People like to talk about themselves, most of the time without thinking. Sometimes they even say things that are detrimental to their own best interests. I had one guy complain to me for the whole 5 minutes about how his previous landlord did not do any repairs, and he's taking him to court. I shredded his application as soon as I hung up the phone with him.

This may seem like a lot of questions, and it might take a lot of time. Just keep in mind that this is a process of elimination. You are trying to get rid of all the potential trouble tenants in the shortest amount of time possible, so ask those questions! I get a pretty good feel for potential renters just by asking a couple of questions, but if you are new at this, it'll take some time to learn this skill.

Some of you might ask how I know if I am talking to a good renter. For starters, good renters have options, so they are a little bit picky. Their income is over the required amount, and they have zero court cases. They ask lots of relevant questions, follow instructions, know the area well, and have driven by the complex before texting me. They do their homework and want to know how to pay rent and how to file work orders. Finally, they want to move in at the beginning of the month since they have already paid rent and given notice to their old landlord. They also don't mind paying a higher deposit because they know they will get it back.

Another rule is never to lower your standards and rent to marginal tenants. I have been tempted many times, especially when I have many vacancies. But I have learned just to be patient and wait for the right tenants; it always works out better in the long run. As mentioned before, try lowering the asking rent and increasing the security deposit in a soft market to attract better long-term tenants.

So now you have made your decision to either approve or deny an application. How do you proceed? Let's first discuss how to deny an application. After talking to the applicant on the phone, you have most likely already decided what to do. If you want to reject the application, say something like, "Thank you for your time Mr. Jones. Now that I have all the information we need, I'll forward your application to the owner for review. We do have a lot of interest in this unit, so it will take the owner some time to review all the applications and get back to you. So please be patient." By saying this, you are hinting that the applicant might not get the apartment due to the high level of competition. The key is to never reject them directly. Just think of it like breaking up with someone in a relationship; you don't ever want to tell him or her that you don't want to see them again. You don't want them to go psycho on you, so you stop answering their calls, and after a while, they hopefully get

Chapter 10: Qualifying and Leasing

the hint and stop calling you. Do the same here! In some cases, the applicant may act like a stalker; they will call you days and nights, demanding to get an answer or their application fee back. In this case, you know you made the right decision denying their application. You can text the following to them: "Thank you for your interest in our apartment. There seem to be a few extremely qualified applicants besides yourself. We'll let you know if anything comes through for you, but it doesn't look good at the moment. Just to be safe, keep looking." As you can see, I am not giving them a flat "no" because I don't want them to go full out psycho on me. Instead, I give them "soft no" and most likely, that will be the last I hear from them. Genius!

What if you decide that this applicant is a good fit? What's next? First, you have to decide what security deposit you want to charge. I usually charge a 1-month security deposit unless they fall into the high-risk category. High-risk applicants include first-time renters, renters whose families co-sign since they don't have enough income, out of towners who just moved to the area for new jobs, students with jobs, and self-employed applicants with bank statements showing income. I charge them at least a 1.5-month security deposit. Every state has a maximum amount that you can charge for a security deposit, so make sure you check your state laws and charge accordingly.

At this point, you can tell the applicant that you have approved their application. I also ask them to get a pen and a piece of paper to write down the number I am about to give them. I tell them to write down the monthly rent amount, how much the refundable security deposit is, and then add those two numbers to get the total move-in cost. Then I tell them that they are approved and ask them what time they can come in to pay, sign the lease, and move in.

At this point, you will get some push backs. They will sometimes set up a time with you right away, or they will tell you they don't have the full deposit or don't want to move in until later. Keep in mind that you don't want to wait longer than two weeks for any new renter. For those applicants that don't want to move in for another month, you simply tell them that you cannot hold the unit for that long and ask them to call back when they are ready to move forward. If they need time to save up for the move-in money, I ask them to come in that day to pay a partial deposit to hold the unit and sign the lease. They can pay the balance three days before they move in. I also tell them that the money will hold the unit and is not refundable if they change their minds. If they do move in, the holding money will turn into the regular refundable deposit.

Please note here that it is OK to keep showing the unit to other potential renters even though you've collected holding fees. There is no guarantee the renter will eventually move in as agreed. And if you find a more suitable renter, you can refund his holding fees and sign with the other person instead. I recommend outlining this in the lease and informing the applicant as well. That way, he knows that it is in his best interest to pay the balance as soon as possible because anything can happen before he physically moves in.

Another thing to note here is that I collect the deposit and the full 1st month's rent regardless of when the tenant moves in. So if the renter wants to move in on the 16th, they will pay for the full deposit and the entire first month's rent, and then I will prorate their rent for the second month. I used to pro-rate the first month's rent to make it easier for the renter to pay, which turned out to be a big mistake. Since it didn't cost them as much to move in, they would stop paying rent altogether the second month. Now I know that if they don't have the full move-in money when they sign the lease, they will have issues paying rent after they move in. I won't allow that to happen under my watch!

Now you have scheduled a time with the tenant to come in to pay the move-in money. You can either go to the appointment yourself or have your helper sign the lease agreement and collect the money on your behalf. Let's say the renter wants to pay the move-in money and move in on the same day. In this case, I would write up the lease, take a picture of it, and then text it to my helper so she can fill out the blank lease precisely the same way. My helper then meets with the renter, gives him all the necessary paperwork, gets the money, and signs the lease. She can give the renter the keys to move in after that. If I have time, I always prefer to drive up to the property to meet and sign the lease with the renter myself. This is because when you meet them face to face, you can look into their eyes, shake their hands, and talk to them. I like to spend some time sizing them up to see if they are genuinely good people with high moral character or someone who will screw with my business after moving in. If you see anything you don't like during the meeting, tell them that the owner

Chapter 10: Qualifying and Leasing

has changed his mind and decided not to proceed. Apologize for wasting their time and send them on their way.

If you move forward with the lease, walk the property with the renter again to show them that everything is cleaned and working. I also tell them that if they have any issues with anything needing repair within the first three days after moving in, they should contact me right away so I can take care of it for them. At this time, they might ask, "Can you install new blinds for us?" "Doesn't the unit come with a fridge?" "Can I paint this wall?" or "Can you get us a shower curtain?" My answer is always a firm "No," followed by "what you see is what you get. You can still change your mind now and walk away. There are no hard feelings." It's better if they change their mind now than to move out after three months. It would be a waste of time to have to turn this unit over again. So far, I haven't had anyone walk away at this point.

You can then take the money from them, sign the lease, give them the Rent and Work Order Instructions, and again emphasize the importance of paying rent on time. I also tell them that the best relationship after today is if we don't ever talk again since that would mean there are no repairs needed and that they paid their rent on time. Most of the time, they chuckle and say ok. This may sound like a weird thing to say to a new tenant, but it works! It gets us both on the same page.

I want to share a couple of landlord horror stories with you, not to scare you off, but to share what I learned. Here it goes.

I once had a two-bedroom that I was trying to rent, and I was considering an applicant. Let's call him George. George works for himself as a roofer. He makes about $5000 a month, and he gave me his bank statements for the past six months showing consistent income. George is 50 years old and claims to want to move into an apartment that's close to his customers. He did not fill out the application completely, leaving many blanks. Since he did not speak English, I had difficulty communicating with him, even when using Google Translator. There are many red flags here: 1) why does he need a two-bedroom when he's all by himself? 2) I can't communicate with him because of the language barrier, 3) there's a lot of missing information because the application is incomplete, and 4) he makes enough money to live in a class a or b apartment, so why does he want to stay in mine? My gut instinct is to reject his application, but since I had more than 8% vacancies at the time, I decided to go against my gut feeling and let him move in. This was when the nightmare started. The night after he moved into the unit, at 3 a.m., there was loud music and lots of banging on the walls. Neighbors also heard a person crying inside. A couple of tenants called the police immediately. It turns out that George rented this place, not for himself, but his son Jose. Jose was just released from jail a month ago after serving time for drug charges, and he had been staying with his parents. Since Jose still had a drug problem, George wanted to kick him out. So George rented my unit for his son, using it as a "half-way" house, hoping that Jose would get rid of his drug habits. I called George immediately as soon as I heard the story the following day. I told him that his son Jose was not on the lease, so he could not stay there. Either he would have to move out now, or I would start the eviction process. And guess what, all of a sudden, George spoke perfect English. He asked for his full move-in money back, which I was happy to provide. I met them both that afternoon and returned his move in money in full and got my keys back. Then I saw the apartment. The walls were filled with holes, about seven in various sizes. I'm guessing he either punched them with his fists or banged his head against the wall. There were also needles all over the unit. I could not believe that one person had caused so much damage in just one night. I was so mad, not at him for lying to me, but at myself. I went against all my own rules and rented to someone I was not supposed to. I had zero self-discipline, and that's disappointing. After about 2 minutes of feeling sorry for myself, I gathered myself together and called my drywall repair guy to get a quote. Long story short, I was able to fix everything and get it ready for viewing within a week. The lesson is to always follow your rules and gut instincts, so something like this will never happen to you!

The second horror story is a little different. A couple with two little boys applied to rent a one-bedroom apartment. My required income for this particular unit was $2500, but their combined income was only $2100. Also, there were four people; they couldn't all fit into a one-bedroom. They would also use more utilities than average, and I would have to foot the bill. When I called them to let them know that I denied their application, the mom pleaded with me that they had no place to stay and started crying over the phone. My heart softened, and I let them move in without meeting all my qualifications.

Chapter 10: Qualifying and Leasing

Another big mistake. They moved in on June 1st, and they stopped paying rent on July 1. They wouldn't answer the door or take my calls. It took me about a month to get rid of them and another month to repair all the damage. People who do not pay rent are the same ones who will destroy your property.

I did not follow my own protocols in both of the above stories, and the results came back to haunt me. I vowed to myself that I would never be that "sucker" again. In the future, I would leave emotions and personal feelings out of all my business decisions.

The renter that wants to move in in 1-2 weeks tends to be the ideal applicant. When an applicant wants to move in immediately, I have to wonder what's going on with their life that they have such urgency. And of course, I will reject applicants wanting to move in a month later because it'll cost me too much money to wait, and I don't know if they will change their minds. The balance I am looking for is when an applicant wants to move in 1-2 weeks from the day I approve their application. Another note here is that there tend to be more turnovers during the summer months. Families usually like to move during summer because their kids are out of school. They also don't want to move after their children have settled into school in the fall. Most people get their tax returns in April or May, so they have extra money to rent a new place or pay the down payment for a new house. For these reasons, expect more turnover during April, May, June, and July. This is important when you plan your annual rent increase. Suppose you have four existing vacancies in April. In that case, you might want to postpone any rent increases so you won't exceed your goal of having less than 5% monthly vacancies. Just something to keep in mind.

My typical tenant makes about $2500-$3500 a month, and I do not accept any tenants making over $3500 a month. People might ask me if I am crazy to have a rule like this. Hear me out on this one. I have found that people with higher incomes generally have the following characteristics: 1) they tend to be very demanding and want a "Ritz Carlton" type of service when they are paying Motel 6 prices, 2) they are unusually litigious, and 3) they don't stay long-term because they have other options. Most importantly, it just doesn't make sense. An average person with that income should be living in class A or B apartments, not my little class C apartments. It just doesn't add up. Either they are renting for someone else or have an ulterior motive, and I am too busy to figure out which it is. I would much rather just pass on this applicant. I might sound paranoid there, and that's ok; I am running a business, and in this case, the risks outweigh the rewards, so the right business decision is to pass.

One final thought is that it's OK to be aggressive when advertising and showing apartments. Still, you need to take your time to review the applications thoroughly. Suspect every blank space and question all documents provided by the prospective renter. Speak extensively to the applicants over the phone and pass on applications if you have any doubts. Your life will be hell if you take in a tenant from hell. I would much rather have a unit sitting empty for six months than lose sleep because of a nightmare tenant. Also, if renters can afford it, ask for the maximum security deposit allowed by state law; this discourages them from destroying your property when they leave. As I mentioned above, good renters do not mind paying higher deposits because they know they will return the unit in good condition and get their full deposit back. Just like a tenant has the right to change his mind before he moves in, you have the right to change your mind before he moves in. If you see anything that gives you pause before he moves in, let him know you have changed your mind and won't continue with the leasing process. Trust me, it's the right thing to do.

CHAPTER 11
Managing tenants after the move-in

"The carrot is way better than the stick."

When managing tenants in class C apartment complexes, or any apartment complex for that matter, I believe in having rules and sticking to them. Be fair but firm, and don't let anything slide when the tenants don't follow the rules. This is the only way to keep a landlord from going insane when he chooses to manage an apartment all by himself. Managing tenants is a science that will take lots of practice. I am going to break this chapter into three sections. First, I will list some principles I have followed in managing tenants. Then I will talk about what new principles I have added after dealing with tenants along the way. Finally, I'll end the chapter with some tenant stories that I think you will enjoy.

As mentioned before, I charge a late fee and a notice fee, totaling $100, if tenants don't pay by 5 pm on the first of the month. It is not about making additional money off the tenant; it's about getting them to understand that there are consequences when rent is late. You want them to think twice before paying late, thus reducing your headaches.

Minimize cash transactions. This is to keep you and your helpers safe. Sometimes when I visit my properties, tenants will approach me wanting to pay rent in cash. I always tell them to go to the bank since "the owner" does not allow me to accept cash from them. The last thing you want to do is carry around a large amount of cash and get robbed. Also, you want to keep a paper trail of all transactions, which will come in handy if you end up in court with any tenant disputes.

Keep firm office hours of 10 am-1 pm. You don't need to be in the office physically, nor do you need to take calls; you simply need to return texts between those hours. Except for AC or water leaks (or whatever you deem as an emergency), only return calls during those hours. Any tenant who calls or texts me outside those hours will be ignored or get an auto-reply of "Office hours are 10 am-1 pm, please text me back in those hours to get a faster response. If your unit needs repair, please submit a work order at the office, and we will get to it within 24 to 48 hours. Rent is still due on the 1st of the month, no excuses. Thank you."

It is important to manage expectations, especially those of new tenants. They might be able to get away with certain things when they live elsewhere. Now that they live on your property, they need to be taught that they cannot get away with anything anymore. These are some of my tips for managing tenant expectations:

1. If they change the locks without my permission, it will be for the last time since it's cause for eviction. They should also keep a spare key with their friends so they won't call you in the middle of the night when they get locked out (if they do this, do not respond).

2. When a new tenant first moves in, I run water in the kitchen sink, bathroom sink, tub, and toilet in front of them. Then I say, "As you can see, Mr. Jones, the line is clear now. If it gets clogged later, you will need to unclog it with a plunger or Drano or spend the $100 to call the plumber. Do not call me or submit a work request for any clogs that you cause." The rule of thumb is never to pay for any repairs caused by the tenants.

3. Every repair request is an emergency to the tenant, but my voice mail will be the judge of that. Don't give an inch, or they will ask for the world.

4. 99% of tenants will interpret your kindness as weakness and keep pushing the envelope until they know they can't push it any further. It's unfortunate but true in almost all cases. They will only respect you when you are firm on all the rules.

5. When a tenant tells you he does not have the money to cover late fees or repair costs, don't believe him. When you start the eviction process, by some "miracle," he will always come up with the money he owes you.

Chapter 11: Managing tenants after the move-in

6. Always take action when a problem arises. Inaction is the same as being complicit; don't enable bad behavior! It may feel like you are teaching kids in a kindergarten class, and in a sense, you are.

7. Once you decide to evict a tenant, show no mercy. Take them to court and use every legal resource you have. Inspect their unit and serve them the eviction notice. Do whatever it takes to protect your livelihood! The only way to get rid of a bad tenant is as soon as possible.

8. If a tenant takes it as far as going to court to fight eviction, he is a lowlife. Do not show any mercy. In reality, having an eviction history makes it really tough for anyone to rent. I once had a tenant who said that having an eviction record was worse than going to jail for murder in the eyes of a landlord, and he's exactly right!

9. Sometimes, a tenant orders me to do some trivial repairs, or he will move out. I reply that I don't respond to threats and wish them luck if they decide to move out. Also, if they ever threaten me again, I won't take it lightly! They need to know who the boss is before it gets out of hand. Remember, it's always better to have tenants who fear you than ones who take you for granted.

10. Always be clear that you are running a business. You get paid rent to put up with tenant's nonsense, and you have zero tolerance for any B.S.

11. I once had a tenant who somehow got a hold of my regular cell phone number and called at 2 a.m. I answered. He wanted to see if I could get him new curtains because his curtains would not close all the way, letting light in that prevented him from sleeping. I said to him, "You have hands and feet; go to Home Depot and get it yourself. Never call me at this number and waste my time like this again, or else I'll evict you so fast it'll make your head spin!" That was four years ago, and since that incident, he has never called me for any repairs and always pays his rent on time. A perfect model tenant if you ask me. I just needed to put my foot down.

12. Never panic when there are vacancies. Just do more marketing, or even lower the rent in some instances to fill those units. Panicking doesn't help

anything. It only causes you to start making bad decisions, and that's the last thing you need.

13. When a tenant asks for an upgrade, try to turn it into a win-win situation. The key is always to get something in return. One of my tenants once asked me to clean his carpet after living there for over eight years. Normally I would just replace the carpet with tile and be done with it. So I said to him, "Mike, I know carpet gets dirty easily, especially when you have those two boys running around the house all day. Wouldn't it better just to change the carpet to tile? If this is something you want to do, I can talk to the owner and see if he would be willing to pay for half the material cost." He thought about it and said yes, he was willing to put up half the money to buy the tiles, and he could even do the installation himself. I told him I'd get back to him later after I spoke with the "owner." I called him up the following day and told him the "owner" was willing to pay for half the tile cost, on the condition that he'd need to raise the rent by $25 a month. The tenant happily accepted this condition. At the end of the day, this tenant got new flooring, which made him and his family happy, and I got to raise the rent by $25 a month, or $300 a year. Now that's a win-win! Especially since I was going to replace the carpet with tile the next time I turned the unit anyway.

14. When given the option, you always want to deal with the wife when dealing with a married couple. No matter what it seems on the surface, the wife is always in charge of running the household. She makes the decisions, and I only want to deal with decision-makers when doing business. This might sound sexist, but it's a fact of life.

I want to share some principles I follow when managing my properties and a couple of stories that demonstrate why these principles and rules are important.

Sometimes an existing tenant asks to move to another unit within the same complex, either because they want more space or because they want to switch to a unit on the upper floor. I usually try to accommodate them if they are good paying tenants. I 1) ask them to pay the additional security deposit upfront, 2) pre-collect the $300 cleaning/repairing fee for their existing unit (but I will refund whatever I don't use), and 3) require that they clean the just-available

Chapter 11: Managing tenants after the move-in

unit themselves and move in quickly. These three steps save me from having to turn the just vacated unit and give me back their existing unit in rent-ready condition. Another win-win!

Many of my landlording friends have asked me how they can avoid evictions and have high occupancy rates. The key steps are as follows:

1. A robust qualification process when taking in new tenants

2. Immediate response to late rent.

3. Ask slightly below market rent and charge a larger than average security deposit. Good renters have money and are looking for good deals. They also won't screw you when moving out because they want their deposits back.

When you first take over a property, you will go through something I call the "Cycle of Cleansing." Let me explain. During the first couple of years after officially taking over the property, about 20% of the new rental applications you will receive will be from people who have lived there before. Most of them left in bad terms, sometimes without giving notice, and left the units in bad condition. Now they are coming back because they know there's a new owner. They submit an application hoping not to be recognized. Since there is no way around that, you should just expect to go through a cycle of bad tenants before hopefully getting to the good ones as soon as possible.

One myth about being a good landlord is that we need to be there all the time for the tenants. After all, the tenant or customer is always right, right? Wrong! That's the last thing you want to do as a landlord. On the contrary, you want to minimize face-to-face contact with tenants and communicate 100% via text. This does two things: first, it makes you look professional; second, it will make your job easier by giving you the time to think about how to handle problems before diving into them.

When dealing with tenants, it's important to say the right thing and use the right words. For example, do not say, "I have to evict you because you did not pay rent." Instead, say, "Well, you did not pay rent, so now you are making us go through this eviction process. If you just paid rent on time, we wouldn't have this problem." The fact is, they have no one to blame but themselves. Unfortunately, most people like to blame others for their own misdoings. Why is this important? Because if a tenant thinks you are to blame for them getting kicked out, they will most likely do something malicious such as punch holes in the wall or worse.

Something tenants don't get along. My rule is never to get involved in disputes between tenants. I was not there, so I don't know the whole story, and it's not fair for me to determine who's right and who's wrong. I'm their landlord, not their judge or mediator. If they don't get along and have beef with each other, that's what small claims court is for. As long as they don't do anything that causes trouble at my property, I leave it to them to figure out. If they don't, one of them will have to move. I tried playing peacemaker once. Big mistake! You can't make everyone happy by standing in the middle of a dispute. I ended up losing both tenants and learned a valuable lesson.

Ensure you have good, clear rules in place. Instead of stressing out trying to decide how to respond to a situation, you just have to follow your own rules 100% of the time. Easy.

As much as I want to figure out applicants, it's sometimes just too difficult to get a sense of someone's character without spending more time with them. I want to share a quick story with you that I call "Little guy syndrome." A tenant had just moved in. He had a good income, no criminal record, and all the right qualifications; the only thing was that he was a first-time renter. But since he sounded OK on the phone and was willing to pay double the deposit, I let him move in. He proceeded to call me at least 20 times in the first week after moving in. He picked out every little thing in the apartment and wanted me to either do repairs or upgrade the unit. I told him that this is no Ritz Carlton and that he needed to manage his expectations. All of that is no big deal. The big deal was that every time I knocked on his door to do repairs, he would open the door with his right hand while holding a gun in his left hand. Very strange, not to mention a little disconcerting! I asked him about it, and he said he just wanted to be safe since he does not know who's at the door. I was floored. Maybe the stereotype is true that little guys have short fuses, and they tend to overreact since they think everyone is out to get them. In any case, I

Chapter 11: Managing tenants after the move-in

was going to overlook this issue, but then he started to brandish his gun when getting into arguments with the neighbors. I politely asked him to leave.

Many times, decisions must be made based on financial considerations. Once, some tenants of mine vanished after living in one of my units for a year. When I checked, I found four construction workers living in the unit that I had never seen before. They still paid rent on time and caused no trouble. Now I had to make a judgment call to either keep them around or get rid of them. I asked them to come to the office to show me their proof of income and asked them what had happened. They told me that their friends, the old tenants, moved out and just "subleased" the unit to them. I explained to them that what their friends did was not legal and that they would have to do two things: 1) pay $100 more per month in rent since there were more than 4 of them in the unit (which would also cost me more on utilities), and 2) pay the security deposit. If they did those two things, I told them I would be willing to sign a new lease and let them stay on. They agreed. The logical thing would have been just to get rid of them. But I figured since they paid rent on time and seemed to be decent guys, I would be better off keeping them around. And it would have been very time consuming and costly to evict them. They have been great tenants for the past three years, so I guess I made the right call!

Since I can't be at my property all the time and don't have any surveillance cameras installed, I had to think of a way to keep tabs on my investments. This is where what I learned in my college psychology became useful. I know most people are noisy and want to get involved in others' business. So I started telling all my tenants to keep their eyes and ears open for me and text me anytime they noticed something going on in the complex. Listening to their complaints, which include things like trails of beer cans, trash, and loud noises, gave me a good idea of what was going on. If I can't identify who the troublemakers are, I just quietly ask around. Most of my tenants are good people who don't cause trouble and just want a safe, quiet place to live. As long as I guarantee their anonymity, they will tell me who the troublemakers are and even suggest how to best deal with them.

My philosophy is to always deal with problems immediately because they'll only get worse if you wait. Most importantly, everyone is watching. If someone has a dog in their unit, knowing this is a pet-free complex, and I don't do anything about it, guess what? By this time next week, there will be two more tenants with dogs. That's just the reality of things. You must train tenants to understand that you are firm on the rules and enforce them 100% of the time. They can follow the rules or start packing. Dealing with the issue of pets is a constant battle. Be firm and stick to your rules; there's just no other good way to deal with it.

I once had to confront a tenant because he was feeding wild pigeons on the front lawn, and the birds were making a mess in my yard. When I tried to speak with him, he pulled the "no speaking English" card. I told him ok, walked back to my office, wrote up a non-renewal notice, and handed it to him. All of a sudden, he could speak perfect English! No more feeding pigeons after that. The "no English card" is also sometimes used when I confront tenants about late rent. I just keep saying, "Donde esta renta" (which means "where is rent" in Spanish) over and over again until they pay. Never let them use a language barrier to excuse not paying rent or breaking the rules. Sometimes the tenant really does not speak a word of English. Still, it is their responsibility to find a translator to communicate with me. They can ask their neighbor or sometimes their kids to translate for them, but I do not let them put that responsibility on me.

As I have mentioned, the best tenants usually work 8-10 hours a day and are rarely seen around the complex. One downside is that they typically give no notice when they move out. They simply move out in the middle of the night and are gone by morning. They always pay rent on time, so if I don't see rent from them by the 2nd of the month, chances are they have moved. I used to get so mad about tenants not giving me move-out notices, but now I am glad when this happens. They leave without putting up a fight, and that minimizes my downtime. This makes my job so much easier since I can immediately start turning the unit and getting it ready to rent. This also goes back to why I always try to collect as high a security deposit as possible. It's essential to gain access to the unit right away after a tenant has moved out due to the risk of bug infestation. If they have left any trash or food inside the unit, it won't be long before cockroaches come to call. I once had to file an eviction with the court to get rid of a tenant. Even though they had moved out two weeks prior, I had to wait for the judge to grant me the right to enter the unit. I was shocked when I entered — there were hundreds, even thousands, of little

Chapter 11: Managing tenants after the move-in

roaches crawling all over the place! Some even fell on my head when I opened the front door. The condition of the unit was just disgusting. They had left food scraps and trash inside, and roaches can smell food a mile away! It took the pest control company an entire week and $850 to eradicate all the bugs. Sometimes, that's just the cost of doing business.

I always tell my tenants that I am just a property manager, not the owner. I tell them that all major decisions need to be approved by the owner first. This accomplishes two things: first, it gives me a buffer and a reason not to respond to unreasonable tenant requests; second, I avoid any significant confrontations with tenants. I have gotten very used to the line, "I am here to help you resolve this issue between you and the landlord, so we are on the same side here." That line has saved my butt many times and made property management so much easier! On another note, never drive a nice car when you go visit a property. The last thing you want to do is have the tenant thinking it's no big deal to pay rent late because the landlord or property manager makes too much money anyway.

"Play no favors and cut no breaks."

That's my motto when managing tenants. People don't change. The ones that pay rent late will always pay rent late. I will just keep charging late fees until one day when the vacancies have fallen below 5% (my goal is to always keep vacancies under 5%), I'll give them a non-renewal notice. The ones that keep causing trouble on the property and giving me a headache will immediately receive non-renewal notices. This all goes back to why month-to-month leases are best.

You will see all kinds of things when you manage a complex. I was once walking one of my properties when I smelled something like gas, so I knocked on the tenant's door, trying to find out where it was coming from. It turns out the tenant did not have the money to pay for electricity, so he was using a generator to supply electricity to his unit. To make matters worse, he plugged the generator into the outlet outside the building, which I pay for! Not only was this setup costing me money, but it was also a fire hazard. I put a stop to it right away. I also had a tenant who used my parking lot to run a car washing business. I had no idea until I got my water bill the next month. It was a thousand dollars over my normal monthly bill! I found out what he was doing after talking to other tenants. When I confronted him about it, he had the audacity to say, "Well, I got laid off from my job, so I had to make money somehow. How else am I going to pay rent if you don't let me do this!" This guy was crazy! Needless to say, he's no longer my tenant. I also assign each tenant either one or two parking spots, depending on how many bedrooms they are renting. Since I am not the parking police, I allow any tenant to call and get another's car towed if it's parked in their spot.

I also do not allow parties. I don't care if it's a kids' birthday party or a BBQ party over Memorial Day weekend, no parties whatsoever. I like parties myself, but I don't particularly like cleaning up after other people when the party's over, not to mention all the strangers coming to my complex and possibly damaging my property, messing up my lawn, or urinating on my buildings. No, thank you!

I have been told by many agents that I can charge higher rent and increase my property value by adding washers and dryers inside the units. I think that's a myth. I don't believe any tenant would be willing to pay more if there's a laundromat just a 2 minutes' walk away. Those big machines also take up space. I'd think tenants would prefer a bigger room to move around in, instead. Also, I cannot imagine how much more I'd have to pay for water every month! Speaking of the water bill, one thing to note is that trying to cut down on the monthly water bill is a constant battle. Watch it monthly; whenever it goes up by 10%, you know there's something wrong. There could be a leak, or a tenant could be wasting water. Find out as soon as possible before it gets worse and remember that the longer it takes to resolve the water issue, the more money it costs you.

A landlord friend of mine has once told me that "there are no bad tenants, just ones who are not properly trained, and that's on me" He is so right! How will tenants know how to behave if I don't tell them what the rules are when they first move in? Why would any tenants follow the rules if I don't firmly enforce them? So I take full responsibility when I have bad tenants. I can either train them by charging fees or get rid of them if they are not trainable. That makes total sense.

Chapter 11: Managing tenants after the move-in

If a tenant is a troublemaker, you will be able to tell within a week of them moving in. You will start seeing problems immediately, and it will not get better. Many landlords I know give this particular renter a warning, hoping it'll get better. It rarely does! My recommendation is to have a zero-tolerance policy. Don't tolerate bad behavior; instead, do something about it right away. Keep in mind that other tenants are watching to see how the landlord handles this mishap. Any mishandling on your part will result in grand consequences. Every little thing matters when it comes to managing people.

I used to rent to an elderly couple who always paid rent on time and had been with me for many years without causing any trouble. One day, they decided to take in their teenage grandson. Usually, I would have no problem with that, but the boy was troubled. He would hang out with known troublemakers, and instead of walking around the complex to get to the main street, they would jump over my fence to save time, damaging it in the process. The first time it happened, I gave the couple a written warning and asked them to pay for the fence repair, which they did. They also promised me they would make sure it did not happen again. As a side note, I always make tenants pay for damages such as broken windows or holes in the walls right away while they are still living there. Don't wait until they move out, or you'll be stuck with the bill since, most of the time, their security deposit won't cover the repair cost. Getting back to the story, after a week, the fence was damaged again. This time I also saw a bunch of cigarette butts next to the damaged fence. I took immediate action. I gave the older couple a 30-day non-renewal notice. Of course, they came pleading to me again, trying to explain what a tough life their grandson had had and asking that I give him another chance. It's not my responsibility to give their teenage grandson "another chance." I will not pay the penalty in the form of repair costs when they don't have their guest under control. I told them that they were already given a warning, so now they had to leave. They moved out within a month, and I have had no broken fence since. Once again, be fair but firm when enforcing the rules. I also know that people don't change, and I do not have to give anyone a second chance or the benefit of the doubt. This is business, and I need to trust my gut instincts.

As a rule, I aim to hand out 30-day non-renewal notices to at least two tenants per month if my vacancies are less than 5%. I keep an ongoing list of tenants who are either troublemakers or give me attitude when I talk to them.

This is pure business. If they have a bad attitude, necessitating that I spend extra time dealing with them, it's just not worth it. I'm better off getting rid of them and getting new tenants who are easy to deal with, instead.

CHAPTER 12
Rent collection

Collecting rent is an art. If you do it right, it is the easiest thing in the world; but if you let your emotions get in the way, it will be a miserable task. Tenants do their best to pay rent as late as possible and avoid paying any fees. At first, I tried to be a nice guy; I believed all their outrageous excuses and let them pay late without charging late fees. Big mistake! Once the tenants saw me as a pushover, everything went downhill. Some people started paying on the 5th of the month, and the following month, they paid on the 8th! WTH! I knew I was doing something wrong. I realized that people would keep pushing the envelope until they had my back against the wall, and nothing would come out of being nice and showing empathy. I had to make a change, so I started enforcing a zero-tolerance policy on late rent and always collecting late fees. Now my collection is 95% by the 4th of the month, every month! I will share a couple of tenant stories below.

I once had a tenant named David, who lived in my complex for a little over a year. David was 22 years old and lived by himself. He was never home because he worked two different jobs, one at McDonald's and another at Taco Bell across the street. He was always polite when he saw me, but he never paid rent on time. He would call me and beg me to waive his late fees (totaling $100) when I delivered notices on the 2nd of the month. I felt really bad for him, working over 12 hours every day and barely making ends meet, so I always waived the fees for him, and he always paid the rent in full by the 10th of the month. This went on for a year. Then something changed. Instead of calling me and asking me to waive the fees and paying on a later date, he stopped taking my calls and waited until the 18th to pay full rent (still without paying any fees). It was like he was dictating when to pay rent and how much he wanted to pay. I was fed up. I filed for eviction when he failed to pay rent by the second of the following month. We went to court, and this guy, who I have been very generous with up to this point, had the audacity to tell the judge that he never pays the rent on the 1st because it is due on the 20th! He said we had an agreement that he never pays fees, and he pays rent on the 20th. Then he gave the judge his bank statement showing he had always paid rent between the 10th and the 20th of the month. I was floored! It was a good thing that I brought the signed lease with me, and I showed the judge that we had a written agreement that he was supposed to pay rent by the 1st or incur late fees. The judge ruled in my favor, and the tenant had to move out five days after that. This is a perfect example of why empathy and business don't mix!

Another tenant of mine named Anthony was a single dad with two super cute 7-year-old twin boys. Anthony worked long hours to put food on the table for those boys, and his girlfriend moved in to babysit the boys while he was working. The first time I charged him late fees, he was upset and came to the office trying to argue his way out of paying the fees. I told him to either pay or start packing his bags since I would be filing eviction papers in the morning. You would never guess what happened next — he began to cry! He told me he had been down on his luck since his wife left, and he had nowhere to go if I kicked him out. I felt sorry for him and waived the fees. Ever since that office meeting, he always had an excuse for his rent being late. The problem was that I kept waiving the fees for him since I couldn't stand the thought of him and his two boys landing on the street with no place to go. The last time he was late on rent, his excuse was that his truck had broken down and he needed to fix it to get to work and make enough money to pay me rent. The very next day, I saw him with a brand new truck he had just purchased. Ha! Now I knew what was going on; he paid for that nice truck with my money! I showed no mercy after that, and he was gone within a month.

As you might have noticed, the common denominator in the above two examples is ME. It's easy to get caught up in emotions and stories from tenants instead of considering the facts. Everyone wants to be a nice guy, and I am no exception. But now I understand that having greater objectivity gives me the ability to make the best decisions. The rules are the same for everyone, and to be fair, I need to enforce them universally, no matter who the tenant is and what ordeal they're going through. Having the self-discipline to follow my own rules is difficult, but it is necessary. The worst thing you can do is let the situation drag on without a resolution. It will cost you money, anxiety, and

Chapter 12: Rent collection

communicate to the tenants that you're a pushover who is not in charge of your own business.

Another tip I picked up along the way is to charge rent with specific decimal numbers that identify the apartment units. For example, let's say my asking rent for a two-bedroom unit is $900 a month. I will charge the new tenant $901.02 if he moves into apartment number 102. This way, every tenant is paying a different amount at the beginning of the month. This system makes it much easier to verify who has paid rent and who hasn't.

Now that you have the correct mindset and attitude regarding rent collection, the hardest part is done. I make all my tenants go to the bank to deposit rent by the first of the month. Then they have to text me two things: a picture of the bank deposit slip with their unit number written on it and a picture of the bank receipt from the bank teller once they have deposited the rent into my account. They can also pay me online via Zelle Quick Pay. Either way, they need to text me a screenshot of their payments as proof.

I wake up early on the second of every month. By 5 am, all the deposits made on the first will be available online. Then I simply compare the bank statements to my records to see who has paid and who hasn't. Once that's done, I write up the 5-day non-payment notices, take pictures of those notices, and text the images to my helpers. My helpers will write up the notices exactly as I texted and deliver them to the tenants. The whole process takes about 4 hours, and then I am done for the day! See how easy it is to collect rent and pass out rent notices if you have the right system in place?

CHAPTER 13
Helpers, Contractors, and Repair Protocols

Running an apartment is all about collecting rent (income) and maintaining the property (expense). Hopefully, the income more than covers the expenses, leaving a healthy profit. I have spent a lot of time discussing how to maximize revenue. Now let's discuss how to minimize expenses.

Each of my apartment complexes employs someone I call my helper. They are a current tenant in the building who has the following characteristics:

- Articulate, friendly, and nice

- Honest, with good moral character

- Home most of the time

- Has at least basic housekeeping skills

- Reliable, responsible, and detailed oriented

- Knows how to take pictures and text using a cell phone

- Observant, can be the "eyes and ears" of the complex

- Has lived in the complex for a long time and doesn't plan to move out anytime soon

Once I get to know this person, I start giving her little jobs here and there. For example, if one of the units needs to be turned, I hire her to clean it for me. Little by little, I will give her more jobs to do, but only one job at a time to

Chapter 13: Helpers, Contractors, and Repair Protocols

start. I pay her an hourly wage every other week. Hopefully, after a while, we will have built up some mutual trust, and I will hire her as my "helper" for the complex. Below is a list of things I might employ her to do.

- Open and close the laundry room daily and keep it cleaned

- Write up and deliver notices

- Basic groundskeeping and repairs within the units

- Inspect and turn units when a tenant moves out

- Show units to potential renters and help them complete the application, and then text me all of the paperwork

- Sign new leases, take cash from new renters, and deposit the money into my bank account (I try to keep this part to a minimum)

I pay my helper an hourly wage when she cleans the units. For the rest, I pay by task. She keeps a log of everything she does, and I pay her once a month. My monthly budget for a helper is about $500-$1000 per complex under 50 units. A couple of notes here. It will take time to determine whether she is reliable and has the necessary skills I'm looking for. It will also take some time to train her to do all of the various tasks. Whenever I feel that someone is not up to the job, I end the working relationship altogether. The last thing I want is to waste more of my time training her and potentially lose her as a tenant too. Needless to say, having helpers is crucial and allows me to manage my complexes remotely! My helper is my representative in the complex and saves me many trips to the property. Another critical point is never to give your helper the title of "property manager." I have done this several times, and as soon as I grant that title, everything changes. She suddenly becomes very demanding with other tenants because she wants to show them that she's the "manager in charge now." She also demands more pay or even a fixed monthly salary. So now I just call this person my "helper." They report to me, the property manager. They also act as a "bridge" between the tenants and me. Suppose I need to get hold of a tenant when he does not pay rent on time and refuses to take my calls. Instead of driving all the way to the complex just to talk to this tenant, I simply ask my helper to knock on his door and put me on speakerphone. This alone saves me at least 1 hour of driving time! As you can see, finding a good helper is priceless, but it's done mostly by trial and error. I may run through 5-6 candidates before I find the right one. Treat your helper well, bring them gifts, or take them and their family out to lunch sometimes. Always take care of your own! At the same time, always remind them that, as helpful as they are, they're a tenant first and a helper second. They still have to pay rent on time, just like everyone else. Also, keep their rent money and pay separate to keep everything simple. That way, they pay the full rent on the first of the month, and I pay them in full for their work with a separate check. I typically pay helpers close to the 29th or 30th of the month in case they need the money to pay rent. It works out for both parties.

Besides doing the basic tasks outlined above, my helper also acts as my eyes and ears on the property. She informs me of any issues or potential concerns I need to worry about (such as strangers on the property, tenants having dogs, hired help such groundskeepers or repairmen not doing their jobs, tenants that move out without giving notice, etc.). Sometimes I even have her change the door locks when constables come to enforce eviction proceedings.

For basic landscaping or odd jobs around the complex, I always try to give the work to tenants who live on site. First, I know they will do the best they can because they don't want to be on my bad side; second, I would rather pay them than some vendor I don't know, especially since the money will help them pay rent at the beginning of the month.

Next, I will discuss how to find a quality repairman when repairs are needed for the complex.

Just like finding a good helper, finding a good repair guy is very difficult. It takes a lot of trial and error. The saying "good help is hard to find" is very true! I first post simple but specific jobs online such as "replacing a toilet," "painting a one-bedroom apartment," or "unclogging a pipe," and see how they do. Many repair guys claim that they are a "jack of all trades" and can do everything. Stay away from them! My experience is that most repair jobs require specific skill sets, and you want to hire an expert who knows what he is doing. Instead of a "repair guy" coming multiple times to fix the same issue, it will be cheaper

Chapter 13: Helpers, Contractors, and Repair Protocols

to hire a specialist to do the job right the first time. Repairs can be categorized according to the list below, in which I also estimate the approximate cost of their visit. The exact cost will, of course, be dependent on the extent of the repairs.

1. Handyman: does most of the minor repairs when I turn a unit. Simple jobs include fixing electrical plugs, painting, drywall repair, cabinet repair, and replacing kitchen or bathroom faucets. Cost is anywhere from $80-$500

2. Electrician: anything to do with the electrical system. Cost is typically $150-$500

3. Plumber: anything to do with the water supply system, sewer, faucets, clogs, replacing bathroom tubs, etc. Unclogging a drain will cost about $120 and replacing a toilet is about $200, including the toilet.

4. A/C Repairman: this can get very expensive. A simple job like replacing a capacitor is $150, replacing a motor is $280, and installing a used compressor will set you back $600.

5. Water heater repairman: $80 to repair the ignitor, $200 to install a used water heater, and $550 to install a new water heater. When a water heater is leaking, you are better off just putting in a used one than trying to find out where the leak is coming from.

6. Appliance repair: Like the water heater example above, it's usually more cost-effective to replace the broken appliance with a used one. Vendors typically charge $120 to $150 to put in a used gas or electric stove. This price includes disposing of the broken appliance.

As you can see, there is a lot of overlap between handymen and specialists such as plumbers and electricians. The rule of thumb is to hire handymen for minor jobs and specialists for major jobs.

Please note that many repair guys require immediate cash payments upon job completion, and most do not provide any type of guarantee. They also tend to have a very short-term mentality, meaning they try to get the most out of each transaction and don't consider the long-term prospects of working with you. Don't be surprised if a repair guy screws you over for a short-term gain. For example, I have been using the same repair guy for the past four years now. His name is Marley. Recently, I hired him to replace a bathroom tub for me. He quoted me $800 to do the work and said he would start on the following Saturday and finish by Sunday afternoon. Since he had done similar projects for me before, I didn't think there would be any issues, so I left for a quick one-week trip with my family. I got a call from him late Sunday afternoon. He said that once he pulled out the old tub, he found that the drainpipe below the tub had cracked, so he needed to replace the pipe as well. That would be an additional 450 dollars. That did not sit well with me. I had replaced the pipes recently and knew that it should not cost more than 200 dollars. He also said that he wanted the whole $1250 in advance because he needed to pay his assistants. Usually, I would never agree to pay for everything before a job was complete. But since I was out of town with my family and didn't think he would screw me since he had worked with me for four years now, I took his word for it and paid him the $1250. That was a giant mistake! I returned a week later to check on the work, expecting to see a new tub installed. Instead, nothing was done. The old tub was still in place, and it did not look like anyone had been there at all. I tried calling Marley on the phone, but it went straight to his voicemail. When I tried calling again, his phone was turned off. So he essentially screwed me and our four-year working relationship over a measly 1200 dollars. It was incredible to me how anyone could be so short-sighted. Long story short, I ended up getting another plumber to replace the tub, who charged me another $750 and finished the job in 4 hours. I never heard from Marley again.

After this incident, I spent a lot of time going over what had happened in my head. I vowed never to get screwed over like that again and set some rules for myself:

1. Always verify the job by seeing it yourself or having the repair guy text pictures showing what he has done.

2. Never agree to pay upfront. Suppose a repair guy needs to buy material. In that case, I would look online to see how much the material will cost and only pay for the material portion in advance.

Chapter 13: Helpers, Contractors, and Repair Protocols

3. Never trust any repair guy, no matter how long you have worked with him. Treat every project like it's a brand new job and treat the repair guy just like you would someone with whom you are working for the first time.

The key to finding a good handyman is to have options. I am continually looking for a good handyman, trying to have as many options as possible. Even the good ones may turn out poorly one day. It's unfortunate, but that's the reality of things. In addition to looking for handymen online, go to places like Home Depot and Lowes in the early morning. Good repair guys are usually there as early as 6 am buying supplies. Go to the plumbing section to find plumbers and the electrical department to find electricians. If I were looking for a handyman, I would look for a guy who's buying a lot of sheetrock in the drywall section and get his contact information. Just like looking for help online, I would give them a small project to start and go from there. It's a good idea to keep your eyes and ears open in the search for a good handyman.

Most repair guys are unlicensed and unbonded, so the rule is never to pay them the full amount upfront, no matter how long you have known them. Instead, do install payments. If it's a big project, set some milestones and pay him when each milestone is met. That's the only way to pay handymen.

For all my projects, I get multiple quotes and use the best quote to leverage the others. Don't be ashamed to do this! Trust me, the repair guy is used to it as well. They expect customers to shop around for the best price, so it always works to your benefit to keep a list of contractors you can call to get quotes. Also, never let one handyman know he's your only option, or else expect to get some outrageous quotes from him. He will take every opportunity to get the most money out of you, no matter what.

Once I decide to go with a particular handyman, I still try to get a price break, even if it's just 30 dollars. Remember, all those little savings add up, and there is usually a large margin in construction, so there is always room for negotiation.

Once the project is complete, I verify that it was done correctly by taking a look myself or having the handyman text me a picture of the finished work.

Then I have the handyman send me an invoice, and I pay him right away. When I say, "right away," I mean on the same day I receive his invoice. I simply do a Zelle Quickpay online, and he receives immediate payment. Nothing makes a handyman happier than getting paid quickly, and he will always be glad to take your calls the next time you have a job to do. By the way, you always want to get a W9 filled out with any repair guy before he starts any work. It is required by the IRS if you pay anyone over 600 dollars within a year.

Some landlords hire a full-time handyman for every 50 doors they own. I thought about hiring someone when I reached 100 doors but decided against it. My logic is that a decent handyman will cost me about $3500 in salary, in addition to taxes and another 25% in insurance, workers comp, and paid time off. Total, he would cost me about $5000 a month. The worst part is that he cannot do all the major repair jobs, so I would still need to hire specialists such as AC repair guys and plumbers. Financially, it does not make sense. After going through my latest expenses, I calculated that I spent a little under $3200 a month on repairs, including the handyman and all the specialists combined! They are all freelancers, so I don't have to worry about paying for their taxes, insurance, worker comp, etc. Granted, I have to spend time coordinating all the repairmen and contractors, but I would have to do that anyway, even if I hired a full-time handyman. I concluded that I am better off just working with a small group of freelance repairmen. In the following section, I will go over how I set up a protocol for tenants to request repairs, which minimizes my involvement and saves time.

Out of all repair jobs, I consider A/C and plumbing issues to be the most urgent. They require my immediate attention. My complexes are located in a western state where the temperature exceeds 110 degrees for 3-4 months out of the year, so having working A/C is essential. As for plumbing issues, any leaks and water issues will need to be addressed right away before they get worse. The last thing I want to deal with is a broken pipe that floods an entire unit and costs thousands of dollars to replace, on top of what it will do to my water bill! Let's use these two kinds of repairs as examples to help explain how to handle a work order request.

As discussed in an earlier chapter, I gave all new tenants move-in instructions when they signed the lease. A tenant is supposed to try

Chapter 13: Helpers, Contractors, and Repair Protocols

troubleshooting the issue before texting me about any repairs. So if I receive a repair request from a tenant about his A/C, I will text back the following:

"Did you troubleshoot your A/C? 1) Turn off for 1 hour then turn back on, 2) Change the air filter, 3) Change the battery on the thermostat, and 4) Set the temperature to above a room temperature of 76 degrees, or else your A/C will freeze up. Please note that when it's 110+ degrees outside, it will take 2-4 hours for your A/C to cool your apartment. Please note that if a repair guy comes and there is nothing wrong with your A/C, you will need to pay a trip charge of $150. Please try the above four steps now and let me know the results. Thank you."

Half the time, that will be the last time I hear from them. Most people want their unit to be cool right away when they walk into their apartment, but that is just not possible. Since they are walking in from outdoors, where the temperature is over 120 degrees, they will still feel hot upon entering their unit. Now that I have told them there is a $150 trip charge if they falsely report the A/C being broken, they will wait that 4 hours to ensure that the A/C is really broken before requesting repair again. If a tenant complains again after the 4-hour wait, I text back the following:

"So you agree to pay $150 if the repair guy shows up and there's nothing wrong with your A/C, correct? Please confirm now so I can authorize the repair guy to come out."

If I get a text confirmation from the tenant, I respond with:

"Ok, please call my A/C repair guy Manny at 555-555-7777 to schedule a time. I have already authorized the repair with him, thanks."

I keep those three texts on my phone so I can easily copy and paste the wording when the tenant makes the initial request. This is how I coordinate repair requests without using any complicated property management software. Now my job is halfway done; I just need to do the following to fulfill this work order request.

1. Text my A/C guy Manny to let him know that Mr. Tenant from apt #123 will be calling him about A/C repair

2. Once the repair is done, Manny will text me an invoice letting me know what he did and how much it cost. Please note that Manny is required to call me and get my approval for any repairs that cost over 200 dollars BEFORE he does the actual repair, or else he won't get paid. That's the arrangement I make with all my contractors.

3. I then text the tenant to confirm that his A/C works before sending the contractor a check. I also note on the check the apt number and what repair was made for my records.

That's it! As you can see, I take myself out of the process as much as possible. I have the tenants call the contractor to arrange the time between themselves. Instead of having to go there myself to verify that the work was done properly, I have the tenant do that for me. This system took me a lot of trial and error to perfect, but I have been using it for the past five years now, and so far, it has worked wonderfully and saved me so much time. You can use the same system for any type of repair.

For plumbing repairs, I use the following three scripts:

"Did you flush big items such as baby diapers, thick toilet paper, or tampons down the toilet? That will clog up your drain. Also, have you tried using Drano to clear up the clog? Remember, if you cause the clog, you will be responsible for it. You will be charged $150 if a plumber needs to come out to snake your drain."

"So you agree to pay $150 if the plumber comes and finds that you have caused the clog? Please confirm now so I can authorize the plumber to come out."

"Ok, please call my plumber Phil at 555-555-1000 to schedule a time. I have already authorized the repair with him, thanks."

Chapter 13: Helpers, Contractors, and Repair Protocols

Some contractors demand to be paid right away. In these cases, I use my phone app to pay them online using Zelle Quickpay. This enables them to receive payment immediately. Also note that I save all my texts with both contractors and tenants. That way, if there's ever a dispute, I can refer back to our text conversation.

Because A/C and roof repairs are usually the most expensive items, I pay for annual maintenance on these systems. Roofs typically require a new coating every 3-5 years, depending on where you live. I also get A/C maintenance once a year. In addition, I provide tenants with an air filter every six months because it helps cut down on the number of A/C units that break down. One quick tip here, A/C guys are usually swamped with jobs during the summer but get no work during the winter. They will often give you a great deal if you hire them to do A/C maintenance in the winter months. I also try to buy extra used A/C parts like compressors and motors in the winter when they're half price. I can then use those parts and just pay A/C contractors for labor when the summer months roll around.

I'm sure there are more things I can learn about handling repairs. I always search online to improve my knowledge of doing various kinds of projects. The more you know, the less you will be ripped off. I understand that what I don't know can hurt me. Since monthly repair costs can be high, I must do everything I can to cut down on expenses. It's an ongoing learning process.

CHAPTER 14
Evictions

Evicting a tenant is the part of the business that landlords dread most because they think it's a long process that involves going to court multiple times. But it does not have to be like that. In this chapter, I will explain all the steps of evicting a tenant. As long as you keep a good paper trail and keep communication open with the tenant, the eviction process is a breeze.

There are only two reasons why a landlord wants to evict a tenant. The first and most common reason is that the tenants have stopped paying rent. The second reason is that the tenant is causing trouble by doing things like selling drugs, playing loud music in the middle of the night, damaging property, or not keeping their area clean. The most critical part to remember about evictions is that you have the "right" to evict any of your tenants at any time. That's why having a month-to-month lease is so important! With a month-to-month lease, you can choose to terminate the lease by giving a non-renewal notice to the tenant you want to get rid of without giving him any reason. He will need to be out within 30 days.

You need to find the right eviction attorney. There is always that one attorney in town who does nothing but eviction cases; find him and build a good relationship with him. The one I use processes approximately 80 eviction cases per day, and that's all he does. You will need their assistance as long as you own property.

You need to have the right mentality and mindset. Always remember that this is business, not personal. The tenant wants to stay here as long as possible without paying rent. At the same time, you want to get rid of them as soon as possible to turn the unit and then rent it to someone else. The power dynamic is interesting here. The landlord has all the power before a tenant moves into

Chapter 14: Evictions

the unit, but virtually none after. Tenants can choose to pay rent or not to pay rent. All the landlord can do to get the non-paying tenant out is to go through the legal process of eviction. The best way to avoid eviction is to stop those bad tenants from coming in in the first place. That's why I spent so much time in the previous chapters on qualifying new tenants. But now, unfortunately, a bad tenant fell through the cracks and is living in the building. How can you get him out?

What kind of leverage do you have against this bad tenant? First, the eviction record will stay with him for 10+ years and make it very difficult for him to get another apartment. Second, you can pay him to leave. Now I will go over the step-by-step process of eviction. Once again, I need to put a disclaimer here. This is how eviction works in my state, and it may be different in your state, so make sure you check with your attorney before proceeding.

Step 1: Give the tenant a non-payment notice on the 2nd of the month if they didn't pay rent on the 1st. Now the tenant has five days to pay rent, plus the fees occurred. Over the course of these five days, call and text the tenant or even knock on his door to demand that he pay. The tenants who intend to pay will take your calls and make payment arrangements with you. The tenants who have no intention of paying rent will not take your calls or even answer the door when you knock. Based on the tenant's response, you can get a sense of who will pay and who will not pay before the five days are up.

Step 2: Day 6. The five-day deadline is up. Try to get in touch with the tenant again to see if they will pay or not. If they say no or if you can't get a hold of them, file the paperwork with your attorney to start the eviction process. There are four documents you need to provide your attorney: 1) a copy of the signed lease, 2) the five-day non-payment notice, 3) a ledger for the last six months, and 4) an attorney's worksheet filled out with all the tenant's information. Once you send these documents to your attorney, follow up with a phone call to ensure he got your email and confirm that all the information is complete.

Step 3: Day 7. The process server has served the tenant with a notice to appear in court. By this time, the tenant will start to worry since he just received an official court document showing that he's been evicted. This is the best time to reach out to the tenant again. Call him up and say, "Mr. Jones, I am sure you have received the court paper today. As you know, it will be almost impossible for you to get a place to rent in the future with an eviction history. I really don't want to put you in that position. So if you would like to move out voluntarily now, I will tell the landlord to drop the case and not proceed with legal proceedings. How does that sound?" 80% of the time I say this, the tenant and I come to an agreement where they move out within three days. If they actually move out per our agreement, I drop the case. 20% of the time, the tenant tells me he wants to go to court, which is fine by me.

One thing to note here is that it's in your best interest to keep the communication channel open with this tenant. I do my best to let him know that I'm aware he's having a hard time with rent and that I am on his side. Since it's the "landlord/owner" who insists on filing for eviction, I am just the middleman. My goal is to convince him to move out voluntarily so he won't have trouble renting other apartments for the rest of his life. Also, since the tenant has not paid rent, his words mean absolutely nothing. Watch what he does, not what he says. In addition, you should never take partial payment from tenants who are being evicted. During the eviction hearing, the tenant can claim that he has come to an agreement with you to pay rent in installments. This would delay the eviction process.

Step 4: Day 14. A day before the hearing, I make a last-ditch effort to get the tenant to move out voluntarily. I will say to him, "Well, Mr. Jones, the court date is tomorrow. Are you sure you don't want to move out on your own to avoid having an eviction record?" and see what he says. Suppose he still insists on going to court to fight the eviction. In that case, I will say, "Mr. Jones, at this time, I can either pay an attorney to go to court tomorrow or I can use the same money to pay you to leave. I'll tell you what. I spoke with the landlord this morning, and he is willing to give you $200 cash right now if you move out by this afternoon. You can use this money to facilitate the move or do whatever you want with it. How does that sound to you?" Half the time, the tenant will accept my offer and move out immediately.

Step 5: Day 15. I appear in the court hearing with my attorney. This is actually the easy part. Most of the time, I let my attorney do all the talking and don't have to speak at all. The tenant typically makes all sorts of excuses for why he has not paid rent. As long as I have all the proper paperwork, including the

Chapter 14: Evictions

notices, the judge will rule in my favor and grant me the judgment. He will tell the tenant that he has to move out within five days.

Step 6: Day 20. The tenant is still not out. I informed my attorney to apply for a writ. Once I obtain a writ, I can call my local constable to enforce the writ and do the lockout. This is where the constable comes and knocks on the tenant's door with me, informs the tenant that he needs to move out now, and watches the tenant move out while I change the locks.

Most of the time, I can get the tenant out by the 20th of the month. I always expect the unit to be badly damaged and dirty by this point, and it takes me about a week on average to turn it and get it ready for viewing. If everything goes smoothly, the timing will actually work out well for me. It's perfect if I can get the unit ready to show by the 27 or 28th of the month because that's when most renters call about apartments.

The cost breakdown for evictions is as follows:

$60	Filing fees
$40	Process server fees
$50	If the case dismissed, or an additional $100 if it goes to court
$180	Writ and attorney cost
$430	Total eviction cost

This cost is why it's in your best interest to keep communication lines open with the tenant and try to pay the tenant to move out asap. The longer the eviction process takes, the more it will end up costing you. You might think $430 is cheap to get rid of a bad tenant, but it costs you way more than that. It will be another $700 to turn the unit since it'll most likely be badly damaged, and you are already missing a month's worth of rent at $850 per unit. So the total cost is about $2000 per eviction. That is a significant expense! This is why the best strategy is to spot the bad tenants before they move in. Of course, it's easier said than done. I'm not sure what the national average is, but for me, owning about 100 doors, I average about one eviction every three months.

Usually, the judgment against the tenant will cost around $1500, including all fees and attorney costs. Some landlords choose to hire a collection agency to try and garnish some wages from the evicted tenant. I prefer just to let it go.

I have spoken to my attorney about whether I should pursue collection and found that it can take up to 3-6 months, with $150 in fees plus 30% of the total debt. I figure that since the evicted tenant can just get another job and there is no guarantee I will get any money back, it is simply not worth it. There are other fish to fry, and my time is much better spent trying to fill the unit quickly instead.

For a tenant who's getting evicted not because he didn't pay rent on time but because he's causing trouble in the complex, the process is a little trickier. For example, say you're evicting a tenant because he's hiding a pet in his apartment. Instead of giving him notice for non-compliance, I'd recommend just giving him a non-renewal notice, for which you don't have to give a reason. If this case ends up in court, it would be very difficult to prove to the court that he owns a pet. It is much easier to go through the route of non-renewal.

Some of you might think it is unfair to offer the tenant "cash for keys" since he already owes me rent. I don't look at it that way. My thinking is that this is a business, and the fact is, I'm not going to get my rent from him no matter what. Now my only goal is to get him out asap, so offering him money to move out is my best option. It will save me time by not having to go to court, and I won't have to pay my attorney additional money. Most importantly, I can get the tenant out that same day and won't have to wait another six days to do the lockout with the constable. The tenant gets an extra $200 in cash. It's a win-win any way you look at it. Once again, this is a business, so look at everything from a business (aka money) perspective.

CHAPTER 15
Bookkeeping and Budgeting

This chapter will cover how to manage a complex by the numbers and describe what type of philosophy you need to succeed.

In addition to recording the collected rents in an excel file, there are two additional files you need to maintain: Monthly Profit and Loss statements and monthly rental tax reports. Each should take about 30 minutes to update.

Let's start with the Profit and Loss Statement. Because I pay all my bills and vendors straight out of my bank account and credit card, it is very easy to track my income and expenses. If you don't know how to make a P&L statement, just google it. You need to do this on your own, don't rely on a CPA to do it for you. You need to know where the money is coming from and where it is going. I also compare my current expenses to those from the previous month to see whether they increased or decreased. If I see my water bill shoot up from $1200 a month to $1800 a month, I know there must be a leak, and I need to fix that problem asap before I lose any more money! This process is what I call "Managing by Numbers." Number don't lie. I typically spend at least 1 hour each month reviewing my P&L statement carefully to see if there are any ways I can make my business more efficient and profitable.

Monthly rental tax reporting is easy. My state requires that I pay 2.5% rental tax by the 20th of the following month. You will need your CPA to help you set up an account online, and then you can just go online after you collect rent and pay. It is pretty straight forward. Do not try to cheat on your taxes! You can make more money by increasing the rent or reducing expenses, but you never, ever want to cheat on your taxes. The IRS is not someone you want to mess with!

Now let's look at budgeting. Once the rent has stabilized and you have shaved as many expenses as possible using the methods outlined in previous chapters, your expenses should look similar to mine.

Percent of Expenses vs. Rent Collected

Mortgage	30%	including property tax, interest, and principal
Helper	6%	
Repair	5%	including handymen, a/c repair, plumbing repair, glass, and appliance replacement
Remodel	5%	including unit turnover, roof replacement/patch, and supplies
Utilities	5%	including outside lights electric, and water for the entire complex
Tax	2.5%	
Insurance	2%	
Landscape	1%	
Miscellaneous	3%	

The total expenses, including the mortgage, are roughly 60%. Deducting 5% vacancies, that leaves me with a 35% profit. Not bad, especially compared to the previous owner, who was only taking home 20% or less in profit. At this point, I still have not raised the rent on any of the units. By reducing the monthly expenses, I have also increased the net operating income (NOI), which significantly increases the value of my property.

Now is the perfect time to talk about annual rent increases. It is important to charge market rates for new tenants moving into vacant units. To determine the market rate, drive around the neighborhood, determine what your competitors are asking, and charge the new rate accordingly. As for existing tenants, it's reasonable for the landlord to increase the rent to account for 5% in annual inflation. For tenants who pay $800 per month, it's reasonable to charge a 5% ($40) increase. For "troublemaking" tenants who give me a constant headache, I would double that amount to $80. That's reasonable since I have to spend my time, which is very expensive, dealing with them on a daily basis. If a tenant chooses to move out voluntarily because he does not want to pay the higher rent, that's another win-win! Most of the time, the market rent

Chapter 15: Bookkeeping and Budgeting

will go up by more than 5% per year, so the new in-coming tenants will most likely be paying more. Yes, I might lose a month of rent due to a vacancy, but if I can charge an additional $100 per month, on a modest annual cap of 5%, my property value goes up by $12,000, so it's well worth it.

As we have discussed in the previous chapter, you want to minimize items inside your units. Only provide the bare minimum for the new tenant. My state does not require me to offer window blinds, dishwashers, or kitchen sink garbage disposals, so I remove them from all my units. You might ask why not keep what's already there. The answer is because then I don't have to repair something that's not there. The tenants who stay with me don't decide to move out because those "extras" are missing; they are just looking for the least expensive place to live. As for the refrigerators, many of my new tenants want to bring their own anyway. Also, the most common reason why refrigerators stop working is that tenants overstuff them with too much food, which blocks the vent and causes the unit to break down. With all the new tenants, I recommend a vendor that I know charges $150 for a used refrigerator in good condition so that they can buy their own. It's theirs, so it will be their responsibility to fix. They can also take it with them when they move out. I haven't lost one single tenant due to this policy, so it's working out well. Tenants get to choose their own fridge that suits their needs, and I get fewer headaches from having to repair appliances — another win-win in the books!

Remember the saying "a penny saved is a penny earned"? It's true! Every penny you save in the expense column goes straight into your pocket, so you want to be a stickler and scrutinize every single expense on the P&L. I have a date marked on my calendar to renegotiate contracts with my vendors. In addition, don't forget to get a new insurance quote every year since it can get expensive. If you just get multiple quotes from different carriers, you will be surprised by how much you can save!

CHAPTER 16
Section 8

There are many myths about Section 8 tenants. I actually prefer tenants with Section 8. With them, I know that on the 5th of every month, the government will send me a check that covers most of the rent, if not 100%. If I use the same strict qualification criteria to filter out potentially bad tenants, Section 8 tenants can be a gold mine. This chapter will go over what landlords should watch for when accepting Section 8 tenants.

When an inquiry comes in from a renter with Section 8, I make sure she has a Section 8 voucher in hand before I even talk to her. There is a long wait for Section 8; even if someone is approved, they are not necessarily eligible right away. The actual physical voucher confirms that they are eligible now. Suppose the renter wants to rent the apartment after seeing the property. In that case, she submits her application along with her voucher and 20 pages of paperwork. She still needs to meet all the qualifications; the only difference is that she does not need to meet the three times income requirement. However, she does need to make at least $1000 a month to cover utilities and food.

Before reviewing her application, I will call her caseworker to confirm her eligibility and determine how much she's approved for and what portion of the monthly rent she has to pay out of pocket. One important thing to note here is that the tenant's portion is not determined by the rent amount. Instead, it's based on the amount of money they make per month. This is important because it means you don't have to worry about the asking rent being too high. Once everything checks out, I fill out the 20-page rental application. I have a partially completed draft of the application that I can simply refer to while filling out a new one. With that system, I can usually complete the application in less than 30 minutes. Another useful tip here: let's say that my asking rent is $1500, but the applicant is only approved for $1250. I still fill out the Section

Chapter 16: Section 8

8 application asking for the full $1500. Every caseworker has the authority to increase a tenant's approved amount. If the price goes over their limits, they will call me to negotiate. The bottom line is, always ask for the maximum amount and don't worry about the application being rejected due to a high asking rent.

Now it's time for the inspection. I always schedule a time to do a unit inspection with the Section 8 inspector. Just be friendly during the inspection and fix anything the inspector asks you to. As long as you do, there should be no problems. After the inspection passes, call the renter to come in to sign the lease and pay the deposit. Then you can give her the keys to move in. Please note that it might take up to 2 months before Section 8 sends you the first payment, but it will include all the back rent since the renter moved in.

Most of my Section 8 tenants are well-behaved, nice people. Once in a while, just like with regular tenants, I do get some crazy ones. In case they don't know, I let them know that I am one of the few complexes in the area that accepts Section 8. If they don't pay rent on time, participate in any illegal activities, or file any frivolous complaints against me with Section 8, I'll not only kick them out but also make sure they can't find another place to live due to my bad reference or see that they lose their Section 8 voucher altogether. This is not a threat. I am just stating the facts, so we are all on the same page.

I want to share a horror story that involves a Section 8 tenant. I once rented to a Section 8 tenant named Monica, who lived in one of my complexes for three years. Monica was 70 years old and a very nice lady, but she had diabetes and had to visit doctors often. I rarely saw her outside her unit and assumed she was bedridden most of the time. Her Section 8 voucher was under her name, and she was allowed to have a daughter living with her. Section 8 paid the whole rent, all $1100 a month. Everything was going well until one day, one of her neighbors called and informed me that the daughter was dealing drugs out of her back window. I asked the neighbor, who was also my tenant, to take pictures of her dealing and text them to me so I would have the proof to evict her. To my surprise, the neighbor got me those pictures within a week. I spoke with my attorney and decided to proceed with eviction, with the cause being her violating the lease by engaging in illegal drug activities. The eviction went smoothly. Neither Monica nor her daughter attended the court hearing. They were ordered to leave within five days, which they did. I did not speak with or see either of them this whole time since they stopped taking my calls and did not answer the door when I knocked. I did not think anything of it; I was just glad they moved without any more issues. Soon after, I forgot all about them until, one day, I got a letter from the Section 8 office. It stated that Monica had passed away six months prior and that her daughter had been staying in the unit fraudulently without Monica being there. Now Section 8 would deduct six months' worth of her rent, or $6600, out of my next payment! My jaw dropped to the floor. I called the caseworker immediately and pleaded my case. I told the caseworker that since I didn't live in the complex, there was no way for me to know that Monica had passed away. Also, since Monica was Section 8's client with a caseworker assigned to keep tabs on her, it wasn't my responsibility to regularly check on her. Finally, if it weren't for me filing eviction on her unit, the daughter would have stayed there for the next ten years, for all we know, since she was living there rent-free. The fraud stopped because of me, and I did everything correctly, but now I was penalized? It was not fair and did not make any sense. The caseworker just stated that she was following the rules. The money would be deducted from my next payment, and there was nothing I could do about it. I was so upset that I thought about kicking out all my Section 8 tenants, but then I calmed down and didn't do anything so rash. I learned a big lesson from that ordeal, and now I watch all my Section 8 tenants like a hawk. I won't let any of them die on my watch, not in my complex!

Because of the financial risks, I deliberately keep the number of Section 8 tenants under 10% of my total units. Section 8 makes all the rules, and I have no say in their rulings; it's crazy. But since the rewards outweigh the risks, I decided to stay with them. I just have to be extra careful from now on.

Websites like gosection8.com are a good way to advertise to potential renters who have Section 8 vouchers. You can contact the Section 8 administrator and post an ad on the bulletin board. You can also keep emails of all the Section 8 caseworkers and do an occasional email blast to all of them whenever you have vacancies. Be careful not to send them too many emails; they are already overworked with an overwhelming number of cases. My Section 8 tenants have told me that I am the only one taking Section 8 in the whole city. So in a way, I am giving back to my community by helping people

Chapter 16: Section 8

with lower incomes have a place to live, and I am grateful to be in a position to help.

CHAPTER 17
Free Vacation Time

When I first started landlording just a few years ago, my goal was to go on a two-week vacation every other month, and I have been able to do that for the last two years. I want to share with you some pointers here in case you would like to do the same.

Before we go any further, I think it's important to explain my philosophy regarding money. I think money is just a tool I use to pay for my vacation every other month, which I find to be very fulfilling.

Usually, I like to keep my occupancy at 95% or greater when I am in town. But when I go on vacation, I am OK with it dropping to 92%. Suppose I am on vacation, and my rental occupancy is at 92% or higher. In that case, I can just turn off my phone or put it in airplane mode for the whole day. I will spend just 30 minutes a day checking my messages and making necessary calls. The only thing I have to worry about is dealing with emergencies such as water leaks or bad A/C units. Other than that, I don't even bother doing anything work-related. I can be wholly relaxed laying on the beach sipping my margarita and don't have to worry about anything at all. That feeling is priceless.

The trick is to be organized and accomplish as much as possible before leaving for vacation.

My vacation is always scheduled from the 14th to the 29th of the month. That gives me 13 days to collect most, if not all, of the rent and start all necessary evictions. I come back home before the 29th of the month because it takes me 2-3 days to adjust from "vacation life" back to "normal life."

The following things need to be done before I get on that plane:

Chapter 17: Free Vacation Time

1. All tenants have paid rent or have made arrangements with me to pay rent, and all evictions have started with non-paying tenants.

2. All my helpers have enough blank applications, blank leases, blank 5-day notices, and work hour logs, and all vacancies are ready for showing.

3. I have the phone numbers of all my tenants and vendors with me. All the leases are scanned and stored in my google drive in case I need to refer to them. I also make sure I have paid all vendor bills before I leave.

4. All repair work has been completed; if not, it will be better to wait until I return. Contractors are tricky to deal with, and I don't want to think about them while I am away.

5. If I have fewer than 8% vacancies, I don't bother posting ads or working during vacation. I can just relax and have fun. "Work hard, play hard" is my motto.

I see vacations as my time to recharge and truly experience this wonderful world around me. I see some of my friends working long hours and making tons of money, but they don't even have time for their loved ones or get sick from working too much. I prefer to do it my way, living in the present and being grateful that I get to wake up every day healthy and happy.

CHAPTER 18
Pursuit of Happiness

Now that you have a system in place, the next time something happens, you can just follow your protocols instead of reinventing the wheel. When managing property, or even going through life for that matter, it's much easier to have a system or a routine.

I go through the same routine every day. It gives me great self-discipline and makes me feel great about myself. This is my schedule Monday to Friday.

4:00 am	Wake up, stretch, brush my teeth, do 5 mins of plank exercises, weights, 50 pushups, go through my daily gratitude ritual, meditate
4:30 am	Two hours of cardio at a nearby park, then shower
7 am-8 am	Rental tasks (Email, return text messages from tenants/helpers/vendors, pay bills)
9 am	Breakfast, then my free time from 9:30-11
11- 11:30 am	Rental tasks (Advertise on Facebook or Craigslist for vacancies, return texts)

I only work in those specific times, one hour from 7 am-8 am, and then 30 minutes at 11 am. Some of you may think I'm crazy and that it's impossible to work like this. I have to admit that I initially had a very difficult time, but setting a deadline for myself and sticking to it worked out great for me. Thanks to the deadline, I learned to work efficiently and get things done in a very productive manner. Every second in those 2 hours needs to be used effectively. It sounds crazy, but once I set the goal for myself, my brain and body just adapted to make it happen. That has been my schedule for the past two years, and I haven't lost a beat!

Chapter 18: Pursuit of Happiness

There are other ways to save time in the area of accounts receivable. For billing and payments, I set up most of my monthly bills, such as utility bills, on Auto-Pay. I need to verify other bills, such as payments for vendors and helpers, before issuing payment. I set aside 1 hour every two weeks to pay all my bills. The Key is to use auto-pay as much as possible. When verification is required, you'll need to take care of it yourself.

Most people want to go into commercial real estate not because they enjoy landlording, but because they enjoy the financial freedom it brings.

As mentioned earlier, I keep a checklist of things I need to do by the 14th of the month to help get everything accomplished before going on my monthly vacation. Because I follow my rules to a T, I can run a very tight ship and get everything done quickly. After that, I have plenty of time that I can use at my own discretion. Anthony Robbins defines financial freedom as "Doing what I want, whenever I want, with whomever I want, and as much as I want." I think that's a pretty good definition of financial freedom. I would go a step further and define financial freedom as "Having the freedom to decide what I want to do with my time."

Now that I have shared with you how I successfully reached financial freedom, the next question is, how do I achieve true happiness?

I read in a book once that the following three things define happiness in the order of importance: health, wealth, and the realization of happiness. Let us examine this statement more closely.

A person can have millions of dollars, but it doesn't mean anything if he does not have the time to enjoy spending it. This first item makes sense. The second item on the list is wealth. While it is true that money can't buy happiness, it sure can make my life easier! It gives me the ability to choose what I want to do. I can wake up at 8 am on Monday and decide whether I want to go back to sleep instead of dragging my feet to work and sitting behind a desk for 8 hours, for example. This second item also makes sense. Now, what is this "realization of happiness" business? Well, it means exactly what it says: something as simple as walking my dog or reading a book can be a source of great happiness. It's all in my mind. I can choose to be happy or to be sad at any given moment. Happiness is a choice that I can make at any time! Having material things like a Ferrari or a Gucci bag may or may not bring me happiness. Experiences like traveling to another country, learning a new language and culture, or a simple walk at a nearby park can be exactly what I need to achieve happiness. It took me a while to realize this principle, and I am glad to share it with you now!

As you may have noticed, I have preached repeatedly in this book that having the right mindset is crucial if you want to have a successful landlording career. For example, I try to never get frustrated over little things, and it turns out that nearly all things are little things! I get at least three or four tenants per year who require me to go through the eviction process. That means going to court, cleaning, and repairing a completely wrecked unit, but that is all just part of doing business. I can complain the whole time or learn from the experience and ensure that I don't make the same mistakes again. You must have the right mentality to stay in this business, and most importantly, to stay happy!

I have learned the hard way never to have a partner in this business. In my experience, most business partners end up separating on bad terms. I wouldn't want to lose a friend or a family member over some stupid money. Also, no one should know about my personal finances, not even my lifelong partner. Everything tends to work out better that way.

Both of my parents are civil servants and were frugal raising me. Because of their upbringing, I always lived a modest lifestyle growing up. Even now, after I have "made it" and achieved financial freedom at such a young age, I still live in the same house I purchased over ten years ago. I have not and will let money change who I am. I also find that buying material things or luxury items does nothing for me; the novelty wears off very quickly. Instead, I am more fulfilled when I go on trips. For example, I traveled to Jamaica four years ago and still remember going to my favorite musician, Bob Marley's house. I sit on the same flat rock that he sat on while making his music, feeling like I was there listening to him play. That's an incredible experience I will never forget and a story I will be telling my friends for the rest of my life!

I believe everyone should have a bucket list. No matter where you are in terms of finances, don't wait to get those bucket list items checked off. So

Chapter 18: Pursuit of Happiness

many people have told me about all the things they want to do and all the places they want to go after they retire. My answer to them is always the same, "why can't you do that now? Do you think you will have more fun going on this adventure right now or when you are 65 years old?" Something to think about. I had many items on my bucket list: living in a castle, skydiving, getting a license to fly an airplane, dining in every single 3 Michelin star restaurant in the world, learning to scuba dive, reading books while sipping red wine by the famous Lake Como, driving a Maserati on a racetrack, among many more. I have checked off most of those items, and I strive to do them all! All the money I splurge doing those things is worth it, no matter how much, because those experiences make me happy. I call the money I spend on my bucket list my "happy money."

When I am not on vacation or checking items off my bucket list, I enjoy just staying home reading. I read a wide variety of books, but I most enjoy books relating to motivation, self-discipline, and any books relating to my business. Whatever helps me learn to become a better landlord and streamline my business, I am all for! I also like to spend time thinking and reflecting on everything that's happening around me. I want to learn from all my mistakes so I won't make the same mistakes again. Whenever I do make a mistake, I am always the first to take responsibility. That way, I can move on from complaining to taking action to rectify the problem. There should be no regrets, only constant learning and enjoyment on the journey we call life.

I met someone during one of my trips not too long ago; he asked me what I imagine myself doing 20 years from now. I thought about it and told him I would be doing exactly the same things I am doing now. Still owning and managing apartments, maybe with a reduced number of units, still taking monthly vacations. I live a good and fulfilled life now, and there is no reason to change anything. I think a person should always strive to live in the present, enjoying every moment. Life is like a good wine; it's best to savor it slowly.

I hope this book has helped others out there to become better landlords. Apartment renting can be a profitable business if done correctly. My methods will not work in every situation, but I hope I have at least given you some ideas that you can use for your business. Good luck, and happy landlording!

If you like what you just read, please share this book with your friends. I would really appreciate it if you could also take a minute to do a quick review on Amazon. Let me know why you like or dislike this book, and most importantly, what I need to work on before publishing my next book. Thank you so much in advance! I hope everyone has a prosperous career in real estate!

CHAPTER 19
Book Recommendations

Here are some books that I have found very useful in my property management career

1. Crushing it by Brian Murray
2. How to make money in real estate in the new economy by Matthew Martinez
3. Savvy Real estate investor by Amanda Han
4. Multi-Family Millions by David Lindahl
5. Best real estate investing advice ever by Joe Fairless
6. Building real estate wealth in a changing market by John W Schaub
7. Building wealth one house at a time by John W Schaub
8. Negotiating real estate by J Scott
9. Landlord Hacks by Tonya Trachuk
10. The new investor's guide to owning a mobile home park by Laura Cochran
11. Landlording on autopilot by Mike Butler
12. Real estate finance for investment properties by Steve Berges
13. Buying and selling apartment buildings by Steve Berges
14. Building a rental property empire by Mark Ferguson
15. Managing rental properties by Heather and Brandon Turner
16. How to make big money in small apartments by Lance A Edward

About the Author

Jason A. Scott is a highly successful entrepreneur, author, private pilot, world traveler, and real estate investor who owns more than 100 rental units. He has achieved much of his financial success by owning residential and commercial real estate. Jason has been in real estate since 2009 and specializes in property management, utilizing his Buy & Hold strategy.

As a business consultant and life coach, Jason has helped countless others realize extraordinary results by building self-discipline and persistent focus. He has also held numerous seminars where he enjoys showing others the power of real estate investing and financial freedom.

A life-long adventurer, Jason spends his time flying his plane and visiting his homes in Asia, Europe, and the United States.

Chapter 18: Pursuit of Happiness

Printed in Great Britain
by Amazon